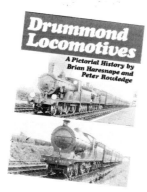
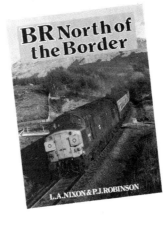

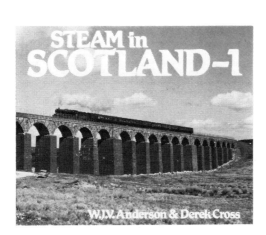
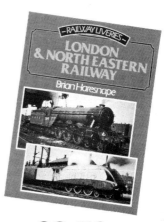

Introduction

SCOTTISH SCENIC ROUTES they are, but although many railway-minded tourists sample ScotRail's outstanding railways in the Highlands and elsewhere with their eyes primarily on natural splendours, it seemed a good idea to produce a 'catch-all' publication that takes the reader behind the scenes. So *Scottish Scenic Routes* is intended to throw light on the whys and wherefores of operating trains over some of the most challenging sections of railway in the British Isles. For so long, despite Beeching and dieselisation, things hung fire. The same trains ran on familiar timings, and to well-established patterns. Newcomers to the lines were frequently incredulous that more was not done to promote the tourist potential of the West Highland, Kyle and Far North lines, just to take three routes described in this book. It was not always obvious at first sight to see why one or another initiative was not taken. Sadly, the resources, managerial and physical, were not always to hand. Most of the routes featured in *Scottish Scenic Routes*

had seen nothing but the effects of rationalisation and reduced resources through the 1960s and 1970s. The same basic railway remained, usually with obsolescent infrastructure, and the opportunity to break out of stalemate was difficult to take. Worse, the possibility of further closures could not be ruled out and this also encouraged an unadventurous approach. By the early 1980s, the climate changed. The Government set its face against further line closures, and the buck was passed to BR. It's yours to maintain, was the message, now find a new solution to retain the lines *and* reduce costs! A formula for operating rural railways in the future was slowly hammered into shape.

The Scottish Region of BR (as was, nowadays ScotRail is the brand-name for rail services in Scotland) has been a pioneer in management organisation, for it was the first to move to a two-tier management: a Regional headquarters to which area managers reported, and a Region where divisions had been abol-

ished. Now ScotRail has two obvious characteristics — a well-spread network and a preponderance of what BR terms Provincial Services, ie those outside the InterCity network and, also, outside those operations attracting financial support from Passenger Transport Executives or else serving London and the South-East. The establishment of business sectors on BR — grouping railway businesses such as InterCity, Provincial Services and Railfreight — had as its priority the vigorous application of a 'commercial, business-led approach. This was set in train in Scotland during mid-1982, and five Area Business Groups were set up, three covering groups of lines. Their directive was to get to grips with the costs of operating sections of railway and services and to relate these directly to revenue generated, with the aim of improving overall financial performance.

Then came a big change in late 1983/early 1984, by which the business-led approach was further refined and ScotRail's say in its Provincial Services was strengthened. As a result, the network of ScotRail lines was split into six sensible geographical/train service groupings, each effectively working to a profit and loss account. Briefly, the six groups are: Strathclyde (PTE supported operations); South West Scotland (as

Contents

Cover:
A perfect day in the Highlands and what better than a day out by train? The 16.05 Fort William-Mallaig nears Banavie on 19 July 1984 behind smartly turned out Class 37 Co-Co diesel electric No 37.264, and Mk 1 stock, with an observation car bringing up the rear. Ben Nevis dominates the scene. *W. A. Sharman*

Back cover:
Steam has reappeared in the Highlands, regularly since 1984 to Mallaig, and less frequently elsewhere. One special excursion was on 20 July 1981 when the Strathspey Railway's LMS '5' 4-6-0 No 5025 worked from Perth to Aviemore, and was photographed in the pass of Killiecrankie. *J. H. Cooper-Smith*

Published by
IAN ALLAN LTD
Coombelands House Weybridge KT15 1HY
Telephone: Weybridge (0932) 58511
Printed by Ian Allan Printing at their works at Coombelands in Runnymede, England

featured in this book); ScotRail InterCity (Edinburgh-Glasgow, Glasgow-Aberdeen, Aberdeen-Inverness, Edinburgh-Aberdeen); East Coast Local (Dundee-Edinburgh and North Berwick local services); North of Scotland (Inverness-Wick/Thurso/Kyle, featured in this book) and West Highland (also featured).

At the same time, area managers were given greater authority and responsibility, including co-ordination of management with engineering departments and so Area Management Groups have been set up. Put crudely, the result has been to establish some areas as almost self-governing sections of railway, and this is particularly true of the Area Managers based at Fort William and Inverness. Their developments are covered in this publication.

This preamble may seem a little forbidding, because management is often the last thing in people's minds as they board a train on a sunny afternoon and look forward to enjoying a run through splendid countryside. But its purpose is to show why observers of British Rail today are excited about what is happening north of the Border. Positive management and imaginative managers are bringing back the colour in the cheeks of Scottish railways, and the public is at last being offered something to write home about. True, some of the equipment remains obsolescent, but on all the sections of railway described in *Scottish Scenic Routes* there are plans for modernisation and improvement.

Readers of *Modern Railways* will have seen editorial features on some of these Scottish lines previously. They have all been updated, and it is encouraging that the material *needed* updating, for proposals have been turned into realities in the intervening period. We hope you will find it interesting reading and, not least, get you out of your armchair to ride on the services. For considerable help in making available facilities, information and advice we should like to thank BR

ScotRail, in particular Chris Green, General Manager, Euan Cameron, Services Manager and George Reynolds, Press Officer, and many other railwaymen north of the Border.

Michael Harris,
Managing Editor,
Modern Railways

Top:
The railway against a backdrop of mountains: on the Kyle line in the late 1970s.
Highlands and Islands Development Board

Above left:
On the Highland main line from Inverness to Perth. A Class 47 locomotive climbs out of Strathdearn to Slochd summit with the 14.30 Inverness-Glasgow on 31 August 1983. *Neil Hargreaves*

Above right:
West Coast main line to Scotland, electrified at 25kV ac: a Class 86 and a Class 87 head the 21.20 Millbrook, Southampton to Coatbridge Freightliner at Crawford on 16 June 1984.
A. O. Wynn

North from Inverness: To Wick, Thurso and Kyle of Lochalsh

Michael Harris

FOR SOME reason, railway publishing in steam days devoted much more purple prose and photographs to the Road to the Isles — the Mallaig Extension — and the West Highland line than to the Highland Railway's routes out of Inverness to Kyle of Lochalsh and the Far North. Indeed, if it hadn't been for the late H. A. Vallance's excellent history of the HR (*The Highland Railway*, pub David & Charles) there would have been precious little in the way of written material on which to rely when travelling to Wick and Thurso. BR's bid to reach John o'Groats is sometimes known as the Far North line and the sparseness of train services has no doubt contributed to the lack of coverage of railway activities beyond Dingwall. The Kyle line has done somewhat better, after all it is the *other* Road to the Isles, and it runs the Mallaig route pretty close when it comes to scenery.

Some of the remoteness and publicity-shyness of the Kyle and Wick routes is a legacy of the Beeching Plan which effectively pronounced a sentence of doom for both. So matters remained, until

the Kyle line very nearly succumbed in the early 1970s. The twilight era spanned nearly 20 years until the dawning of a more hopeful environment, one that should ensure the future of the 232 route miles of railways north and northwest of Inverness.

The Highland lines generally — and certainly those to Wick/Thurso and Kyle — have benefited from ScotRail's stream lined and undoubtedly more responsiv management of the last few years. Th Area Manager, Inverness — currently Bil Wood — has been encouraged to pursue a more positive and independent line s that local opportunities for developing traffic can be speedily taken up. The join BR/HIDB statement on the future of al.

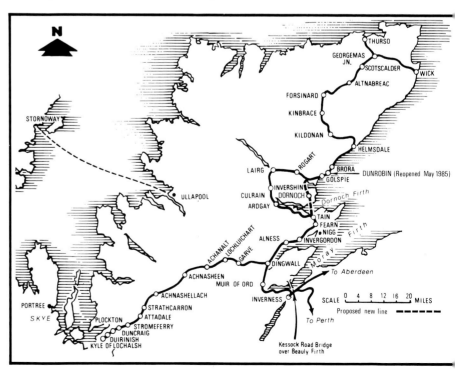

Above:
In the evening of a tranquil autumn day, Class 37 No 37.184 skirts Loch Carron, after departure from Kyle of Lochalsh with a charter train on 25 September 1982. *Colin C. Hall*

Highland lines has therefore proved to be a landmark: it has represented a regional and national commitment to a long-term role for the area's railways after nearly 20 years of uncertainty, and it has also coincided with ScotRail's own determination to tailor its management to suit local characteristics and make the most of the resources to hand.

When the Beeching Report was published in 1963, two aspects of today's perspective were lacking. The Highlands and the north of Scotland had seen a steady depopulation for at least the two previous generations. There was little prospect of establishing new industries and, by so doing, help to stem emigration. The situation started to change during the 1960s and, for all its mixed blessings, the exploitation of North Sea oil and the development of support industries helped to establish a new industrial base, so encouraging people to stay to work in the north of Scotland or move into the area. Unhappily, Britain's declining economy has recently thrown much of such optimism to the winds, although Highland Region resisted the onset of recession until late 1981/early 1982.

The second influence absent in 1963 was the Highlands & Islands Development Board. This body was set up in 1965 to 'enable the Highlands and Islands to play a more effective part in the economic and social development of the nation'. The HIDB has been an effective catalyst and doughty fighter and has done much to promote the creation of an integrated and modernised transport system in the Highlands. The HIDB makes no secret of its determination to ensure retention of the railway system north of Inverness and contributed a submission to the Serpell Committee on the subject. Compared with

the early 1960s, then, there is now vastly more effective lobbying, aided by the creation of the Highland Regional Council in 1975, with specific powers to evolve public transport plans within its area.

But what have the regional bodies achieved towards getting a better deal for the railway routes beyond Inverness? A major initiative was launched early in 1981, when the then HIDB chairman, Sir Kenneth Alexander, met Sir Peter Parker, the current BRB Chairman, and made what HIDB officers have designated a 'crucial contact'. The HIDB had sensed BR's concern at maintaining the rural railway in the face of Whitehall's constantly tightening cash limits. Sir Kenneth suggested a study to evaluate the contribution made by BR lines to the economic and social well-being of the Highlands. Sir Peter picked up the baton, and not only offered to contribute to the study but also agreed to meet a third of the study's costs. Against competitive bids from other consultants, Transportation Systems & Market Research Ltd (the BRB consultancy subsidiary commonly known as Transmark) was awarded the task. As a result of its report, a statement outlining a development programme for the Highland railways was issued by BR and the HIDB just before Christmas 1982. The programme concluded that the costs of closing the Highland lines would be greater than the costs of retention in the short- and medium-term. However, the financial performance of some 'peripheral sections was noted as giving cause for concern'. Actual resolve was translated into a cost-reduction exercise (use of new signalling systems) and greater promotion to increase public awareness of rail services. To Robert Cowan, the new HIDB Chairman, the study itself 'is a sound

justification for the continuation of Highland railway lines . . . [but] sufficient financial resources will have to be made available to BR to support the costs they bear in operating the lines'.

What has been achieved so far? Radio Electronic Token Block (REBT) signalling is now in operation on the Kyle line and will shortly be extended north from Dingwall, so permitting reductions in operating costs and, equally important, greater flexibility in operations. There have been innovations in train operations: freight conveyed on passenger services, and more summer tourist facilities on the Kyle line. Schedules to Thurso and Wick have been pared — necessarily so in view of increasingly attractive road passenger services. The immediate future promises new rolling stock in the shape of Class 150 diesel multiple-units.

To act as a catalyst for commercial development of ScotRail's services, a Commercial Officer at Inverness was appointed in spring 1984 to look at passenger, parcels and freight traffic in the HIDB area, and pass on intelligence of potential rail carryings to the line management so that effective action could follow.

Competition from other modes

There is no doubt that the transport infrastructure in the Highlands has changed dramatically since the early 1960s, and in a way that provides a greater challenge to rail services than almost anywhere else in the British Isles. The great white hope of the Scottish

Left:
Road competition: the Kessock road bridge across the Beauly Firth can be seen in the background as Class 37 No 37.017 approaches Inverness, at Clachnaharry, where the railway crosses the Caledonian Canal, with the 06.35 from Wick/Thurso on 13 June 1984. *A. O. Wynn*

Development Department has been the rebuilding of the A9 trunk road north of Perth up to and including the crossing of the Cromarty Firth. One notes a marked hesitation to put a definite figure on the cost of this programme, effectively completed in September 1982, but it is not unadjacent to £250million. That may be put alongside BR Scottish Region's *overall* investment totalling £18.6million in 1981 and £8.6million in 1982. What is more, the A9's transformation was planned with not even a backward glance as to what it might do for a rail network beyond Perth scarcely flushed with investment since Victorian times. The result has been to make road passenger and freight carriers able to compete with — and improve on — rail times. Combined with 'deregulation' of long-distance coach services under the 1980 Transport Act, BR is immediately up against a problem of service quality. In an aside one might quip, 'not before time'. A better road is one thing, but so far as the rail routes beyond Inverness are concerned, it is also a question of distances by road being slashed. August 1982 saw the opening of the Kessock Bridge at Inverness with the result that the A9 towards Wick now runs across the Black Isle, as well as taking advantage of the 1979-built bridge across the Cromarty Firth.

The Kessock Bridge and the greatly improved road across the Black Isle will be followed by the construction of a bridge across the Dornoch Firth, to cut out the A9's present detour beyond Tain via Bonar Bridge. ScotRail's reaction to the new road crossing could have chosen from three options: do nothing (and watch the Far North line decline), come up with an all-singing, all-dancing scheme for a rail crossing which risked being dismissed, or taking a more reflective, and long-sighted line. The last option was followed and, with political interests supporting a road *and* rail crossing of the Firth, a working party was set up by ScotRail in mid-1984 to look into the

ramifications of the road bridge and its effect on the Far North line. The principle adopted was to make sure that whatever case was presented couldn't be discounted on economic or technical grounds.

Consultants Stewart Wilson & Kilpatrick were appointed to study the technical feasibility of a combined road/rail bridge across the Dornoch Firth while ScotRail's market researchers considered the effect on rail if the road bridge were to open without an alteration to the rail route. There were meetings with the HIDB and Highland Regional Council to explain ScotRail's approach. By February 1985, ScotRail's Executive Group received the consultants' report that a combined road/rail bridge and associated new rail route were perfectly feasible. Most likely to materialise is the construction of 15 miles of new single track railway between Tain and Golspie, with a rail track on the A9 bridge, and a new station

at Dornoch. This would reduce the Inverness-Thurso/Wick rail route by 45 miles and cut journey times appropriately. Also being examined is the possibility of retaining the existing rail line via Ardgay (the former Bonar Bridge station) and Lairg.

Not only does the railway make a detour along the south shore of the Beauly and Dornoch Firths, but, north of Helmsdale, the builders of the Wick line took the route inland to avoid fearsome gradients along the Caithness cliffs. In the latter case, the cost was an extra 23 miles travelling by rail, compared with the route taken by the road between Helmsdale and Wick. Nowadays, with the A9 striking across the Black Isle and over the Cromarty Firth, Wick is only 114 miles from Inverness by road, against the train's 161½ miles; express coaches undercut the rail journey by 1hr. The importance of the rail/road bridge over the Dornoch Firth need hardly be stressed.

Road improvements have had their effect on the competitiveness of the Inverness-Kyle line too. The A890 from Achnasheen to Kyle has been greatly improved, although it remains unfenced. But Highland Omnibuses' service running

Below:
Forging inland north of Helmsdale, at Kilearnan, near Kinbrace is the 11.40 Inverness-Wick/Thurso behind Class 37 No 37.035 on 10 August 1983. *D. M. May*

over the route Inverness-Kyle-Portree via the A82/A87 roads has been speeded up, thanks to road improvements, to give a 2hr 10min run to Kyle, which compares favourably with BR's best of 2hr 40min. The mileage in both cases is about the same. Air services have been greatly stimulated by North Sea oil industry activity, although the scheduled times are influenced by the home base of operations, often restricting their usefulness. These days, Wick enjoys through flights from Glasgow, Aberdeen and Edinburgh.

The freight market

Improvements to the road infrastructure naturally benefit road freight, too. Speedlink air-braked rail freight services were only implemented to/from Inverness at the end of 1982.

Late July 1982 saw the failure of last-ditch attempts to rescue the 10-year old Invergordon aluminium smelter, which ceased operations the previous year. With the death of the smelter went freight business worth £500,000 annually to BR. The slowdown in the exploitation of North Sea oilfields has also reduced the likelihood of any new freight traffic being generated by way of trainloads that might contribute to operating costs into and out of Inverness. Before Invergordon's demise, setting properly attributable revenue against *avoidable* costs, the lines north and west of Inverness did better than break-even.

Operational difficulties

Together with the West Highland lines, the Wick and Kyle routes probably constitute the toughest proposition in operating terms of any section of BR's network. Some of the major challenges are all too easily overlooked. The basics are: a considerable extent (232 route miles) of single-track railway on gradients that are often severe (their effect compounded by sections with fiercesome curvature), involving numerous speed restrictions, and, latterly, slacks for unmanned crossings. The lines thread sparsely populated countryside which experiences really extreme weather in wintertime — snowploughs and the emergency rations carried on passenger trains are not for effect. January 1984 saw a Far North train snowbound north of Helmsdale. Radio communication with the stricken train represented a great improvement on the difficulties of locating a similar casualty in 1978, but drew attention to the need to improve further the on-train aids so as to permit speedy pinpointing by rescue helicopters. As a result, train drivers now have high-visibility arctic apparel and flares are carried to guide helicopters should a train become trapped.

Add to such an impressive catalogue of disadvantages the need to maintain connections out of Inverness, with adequate margins to cater for delays on mainline services possibly 500 miles distant, as well as the necessity to offer portions to both Wick and Thurso on Far North trains, and the restrictions on

operation are obvious. The use made of the passenger services for postal traffic and the disparity of carryings as between summer and winter present further difficulties.

There is little prospect on the Wick line of raising maximum line speeds significantly. The main benefit has come from easing permanent local restrictions, made possible in view of the relatively light traffic density. In all, there are about 32 miles of the Inverness-Wick route, made up of 13 locations, where the Chief Civil Engineer has given the operators a relaxation of 5-10mph on the present limit. In combination with the more powerful Class 37 locomotives, which can accelerate away from slacks more effectively, the line-speed improvements have given savings of about 10min. Speaking of track, ScotRail operators dismiss suggestions of a prospect of deteriorating track on the Wick line due to BR's prevailing financial stringency. Compared with blacklisted routes elsewhere, they counter that the Highland railwaymen have used their ingenuity and so maintain the permanent way in good order. A policy of spot-resleepering is being followed. For 1984/5, restrictions were relaxed over level crossings where 'stop and proceed' arrangements apply, as shown in the accompanying table. The target of timetable accelerations was to achieve a 4hr timing for all Inverness-Wick trains (it is of interest that this time was a feature of one return service in the immediate post-dieselisation period).

However, acceleration of train schedules on both routes has been just one aspect of an improved package. Connections are all-important in areas with sparse public transport. The linking of both services into the Scottish basic interval timetable gave some benefits, such as a good connection into the 17.35 to Wick and 17.55 to Kyle out of the 08.00 King's Cross-Edinburgh/08.10 Birmingham-Edinburgh/13.22 Edinburgh-

Inverness. One innovation for summer 1983 was a Sunday service on the Kyle line, completing the introduction of Sunday services on all routes radiating from Inverness.

Radio communication

Developments in train control and signalling have helped to lift the Kyle and Wick routes into the forefront of railway technology in a bid to improve service quality and cut costs. The severe blizzard that struck north-east Scotland in January 1978 resulted in destruction of most of the overhead pole and wire route over the 59 miles between Lairg and Forsinard. Rather than replace like by like, the British Railways Board, Derby Research & Development Department engineers and Scottish Region staff decided to design a new radio communication system.

So, instead of perpetuating the wire connection between signalboxes, with the transmission of bell-code messages, a system was installed whereby there is

---

Relaxation of speed restrictions over level crossings

From May 1984

Location	Formerly/now
Bunchrew	10mph/45mph (down), 50mph (up)
Delny	25mph/50mph
Halkirk	10mph/50mph
Watten	10mph/30mph (down), 55mph (up)
Hoy	10mph/40mph

From May 1985

Kirkton	25mph/55mph
Kildonnan	STOP/10mph

Below:
Radio signalling (REBT) at Achnasheen on the Kyle line. The notice on the left reads: Stop. Obtain token and permission to Proceed. Class 37 No 37.261 slows for the station stop with the 11.10 Kyle-Inverness on 23 November 1984.
Alex Dasi-Sutton

Left:
With Loch Dùghail in the background, the 09.30 Inverness-Kyle negotiates the manually operated Balnacra crossing behind Class 37 No 37.025 on Sunday, 12 August 1984. *M. M. Hughes*

Radio signalling

The Kyle line is the pilot scheme for the radio-based signalling system developed by the BR Reseach Department, Derby and it was commissioned beyond Dingwall in September 1984. This is the scheme that has featured in the BRB's general proposals for modernising rural railways. Before radio signalling, the 64 mile single-track Dingwall-Kyle of Lochalsh section had three intermediate stations staffed for signalling purposes. There were also four crossing-keeper controlled level crossings, two (at Dingwall) under control of one man. The application of a radio electronic token system on the Kyle line saw removal of all conventional signalling and existing open wire communication circuits. Movements are regulated by a signalman at a control centre in Dingwall. Three level crossings have still to be automated. The limits of single-line working are defined by the provision of stop boards, protected by advance automatic warning system magnets. Train working over the Kyle line is confined to those locomotives fitted with radio and cab displays. Authority for a driver to occupy any single-line section is by a radio transmitted data telegram issued by Dingwall centre, backed up by the transmission of a wire message. On receipt of the message, the limits of authority to proceed are shown on the cab displays. The control centre equipment (BR's first solid state interlocking restricts the electronic issue of 'section authorities' to one per section, in compliance with the block section principle. A figure of around £500,000 is put on th savings to be realised by the implemen tation of the radio electronic token system, against installation costs o £440,000, taking staff reductions and avoidance of the replacement of th dilapidated existing pole route int account. This scheme and the radi communication system are highlighted i the BR/Highlands & Islands Developmen Board report as desirable features to b extended elsewhere on Highland rail ways. Radio signalling will have bee extended north of Dingwall to Wick an Thurso by October 1985 at a cost o £850,000 or so.

The north of Scotland was the test-be for the Open Station system. The pic neering scheme introduced on 2 Novem ber 1981 included Inverness (now completely open station) and all station to Kyle, Wick and Thurso (inclusive Taken with the electronic token system t

radio speech connection between the train control office in Inverness and signalboxes, as well as between Control and locomotives. The £160,000 scheme covers 103 miles of the Far North line between Tain and Georgemas Junction, and was commissioned in August 1980. Eight signalboxes are involved. A transmission unit in the offering signalbox effectively converts the bell-code signal into a radio signal, which is then converted to current at the receiving signalbox and so operates the bells and indicators. Normal speech can be conducted over the radio link from Control to signalboxes and locally-based locomotives are each fitted with an aerial and a transmitter/receiver set. A portable transmitter/receiver is carried on a 'visiting' locomotive working over the Far North line. In addition, road and on-track vehicles belonging to the Signalling & Telecommunications and Chief Civil Engineer's departments are fitted with radio communication equipment which, as on the locomotives or in signalboxes, switches on automatically when a call is received.

The system has worked well and, quite apart from proving its worth in replacement of the pole route, has benefited operations. Local weather conditions can be reported to Control or to drivers of trains, the replacement of an ailing or failed locomotive is made earlier and

quicker (the time taken to obtain assistance has been cut by half), and the system has even allowed a diagnosis of locomotive problems to be relayed over the radio to the enginemen. The need to communicate directly with a train was highlighted when a Far North passenger train was snowed in near Altnabreac in the extreme conditions that destroyed the pole route in the winter of 1978. Difficulties in radio communication come from instances of 'black-spots' in steep cuttings, or when a locomotive has stopped under a bridge.

Besides the Far North line, Inverness Control takes in all 450 route-miles of the Highland system north of Stanley Junction (between Perth and Dunkeld), and also the Aberdeen line eastwards as far as Inverurie. Combine that with the fact that it is the only integrated Control and Total Operations Processing System office on British Rail, as well as noting its inclusion in BR's National Radio Plan — and it is clear that Inverness has brought control and information technology (including dot matrix boards and visual display units displaying passenger train information on the station concourse) to a level probably unparalleled elsewhere on the less-intensively worked areas of BR. In addition, since May 1982, there has been direct speech communication between locomotives and Inverness Control on the Kyle route.

Left:
Dropping down from County March summit on 1 September 1984 is the 12 noon Wick/Thurso-Inverness behind Class 37 No 37.017. *Rod Muncey*

be introduced on the Kyle line and the radio communication scheme, a picture emerges of the sort of operation that may be expected for many of BR's rural railways in the future.

The Wick/Thurso line

Beyond Inverness, the Wick and Kyle lines are regarded as serving different roles. BR talks of the Wick/Thurso services as 'strategic transport', a vital part of the region's transport infrastructure. The trains *were* used reasonably heavily as far as Tain, but the opening of the Kessock Bridge and the improvement of bus services prompted a fall in passenger traffic of some 30%. Nonetheless, the line's social role is pre-eminent, underlined by its excellent record in remaining open in snowy conditions, as compared with the road links. The majority of passengers carried are on through journeys (the average trip was 63 miles in 1981), the service comprising three trains a day each way. An innovation from 26 March 1985 has been an early morning Invergordon-Inverness 'commuter' train, using stock allocated to Inverness for special work. On Sundays, there is a return working to Lairg only, extended as from 1979 to/from Wick in summer.

Passengers joining or alighting at stations beyond Inverness account for 180,000-200,000 journeys annually. An increasing travel market saw rail increase carryings by just under 12% over the 1977-80 period, with a small decline in 1981. The 1984 passenger journey total was 199,600, with a 63/37% split between 'indigenous' and summer (tourist) traffic.

In June 1960, 20 of the wayside stations between Inverness and Wick were closed. Two have since been reopened, Muir of Ord on 4 October 1976 (using the existing station buildings), and Alness (with Portakabin facilities) on 7 May 1973. Alness serves estates which house many Invergordon workers. Also, from 13 May 1985, the private station at Dunrobin (to serve Dunrobin Castle) was opened to passenger traffic; 1984 saw the start of rail-based tours to the Castle, and passengers can now travel to nearer the Castle. The additional stops and introduction of severe slacks at crossings resulted in the Inverness-Wick overall timings marginally deteriorating in the 1970s. The average overall timing both ways of 4hr 48min in 1975/76 was reduced to 4hr 44min in 1980, and to 4hr 21min in May 1982 with the diagramming of Class 37s to the service. The 1983/84 service average was 4hr 11min, and the 1985/86 average timings are 4hr 02min.

Mail traffic results in four of the six trains being Post Office controlled. Red Star parcels are mostly worked on one train each way, connecting with services from the south, while the withdrawal of the Collection & Delivery parcels service, far from seeing a reduction in traffic, has resulted in PO parcels post increasing significantly; the demise of C&D business effected no staff savings.

Above:
Near Loth, between Helmsdale and Brora: the 12 noon Wick/Thurso-Inverness of 11 August 1984: the Class 37 is No 37.260 *Radio Highland*. The locomotive carries the Highland Rail stag's head motif and special livery to commemorate the launching of the Kyle line radio signalling.
D. M. May

The Wick/Thurso passenger service is worked by three Class 37s on the through trains with a fourth on the Thurso 'branch'.Passenger stock, so often the butt of critics of the Far North line, at present consists of late 1950s Mk 1 open second-class stock, some vehicles partially refurbished, and all vacuum-braked and steam heated. Steam heating requires that all locomotives be worked by two men. First-class facilities were withdrawn as from 5 January 1981. The catering service provided on all six trains is restricted to open seconds or brake open seconds with former IC125 trolleys, the attendant switching from northbound to southbound trains midway on the route; consequently, catering is restricted to the southern part of the journey only.

On the face of it, the Wick/Thurso service could be covered by two sets of coaches, but due to the doubtful reliability of the Mk 1 stock three sets are used. In all, about 30 Mk 1 vehicles are allocated to Inverness to cover both routes. Their general state is certainly no worse than Mk 1s of similar age, but they are admittedly unappealing by current standards. The Mk 1 stock, hauled by Class 37/4s, will continue until Class 150 'Sprinter' DMUs become available.

The Kyle line

The tenacity of the Highlanders and the fact that the Kyle line is a comfortable

600-650 miles from London were probably contributory factors to its survival into the 1980s. Back in December 1970, the then Minister of Transport talked of 'not being justified in continuing beyond 1971' the grant for the Kyle service paid under the 1968 Transport Act. Undaunted, the Kyle line outlived that particular warning, and it has survived the transfer from Kyle to Ullapool of the mainland base for the Calmac vehicle ferry service to Stornoway on the Isle of Lewis. However, it is now almost entirely a tourist railway, with relatively few regular local users; in 1981, only 45,000 passenger-journeys were generated at stations between Garve and Kyle inclusive. Nonetheless, this was a marginal improvement in business over 1979/80. But the real worth of the line is in its

Below:
The pretty station building at Plockton, famed for its mild climate, is seen in June 1978, with Class 26 No 26.024 (former motive power type on the Kyle line) on the morning train from Inverness.
M. Soden

tourist potential — overall 75% of passengers carried are on through journeys, many of course on Britrail or HIDB Travel passes. The split between 'indigenous' and summer traffic is 45% to 55%, and total passenger journeys made in 1984 were 77,000. An observation saloon has been hired from Steamtown, Carnforth, and is conveyed on one return journey Mondays-Saturdays June-September; a supplement is payable for travel in this vehicle. The marketing of the saloon has been a success. A recent development is a Sunday service in the summer, first introduced in 1983.

In the past, the broad-brush BR economic approach had made it impractical to cater for peak-season tourist traffic on the Kyle line; it was no secret that business was effectively turned away. Early in 1985, six Mk 1 coaches arrived at Inverness, categorised as marginal stock scheduled for limited use and hence they will not attract the same costs as vehicles on day-in/day-out diagrams. These coaches have been spruced up internally and will be used on midweek Kyle excursions in competition for the 'coaching' market. Also new will be the 'Royal Scotsman' tour train, a private venture enjoying ScotRail's enthusiastic support.

The Kyle line is 'vital' and 'a major tourist attraction' in the view of Highland Regional Council's Transport Officer, Archie Roberts. This is despite the completion of improvements to the A890 road west of Achnasheen in 1977/78. However, this road remains unfenced, with open grazing along its length; a local commentator described attempts to run trials with an express bus in replacement of the train as a 'fiasco'. Such is the concern to maintain the railway to Kyle that the HRC refuses to subsidise Highland Omnibuses' service 18 from Inverness to Kyle via Glenmoriston. Speed is arguably a case for improvement; even with a Class 37,the end-to-end average on a special limited-stop excursion is only 30mph — pleasant though that may be for less impatient tourists.

Freight traffic

Much of the criticism directed at BR for its alleged failings in serving the north of Scotland in the last couple of decades related to freight traffic. The days were, they say, when trains pulled out of Lairg filled with sheep off to winter in the south . . . and then there was the fish traffic from Wick. True enough, even a half-hour's wait at Brora alongside the A9 is proof that the road hauliers have no difficulty in finding business. But what happened north of Inverness merely reflects what many will claim was wrongheaded handling of BR's freight business in the 1960s/early 1970s. By the early 1980s, little other than domestic coal and seasonal fertiliser traffic travelled down the Kyle line. The Howard Doris oil rig yard at Stromeferry saw construction materials initially brought in by rail, but that was all. Household coal (and fertiliser) comprised what little freight business there was north of Brora on the Wick line, catered for by a twice-weekly return working to/from Georgemas Junction. This was the last remnant of the wagonload freight business and from 1984 coal was handled at the concentration depot at Inverness, fed by Speedlink services. The Regional Freight Manager was adamant at this time that BR had an open mind on the retention of freight services to the north: 'We shall struggle to ensure the retention of a freight service to Wick — we haven't washed our hands'. During 1983, there were the first transits of freight containers from Aberdeen to Wick travelling throughout on passenger trains; a notable breakthrough in combined services. More recently, there have been trial loads of peat from Georgemas Junction to Invergordon. There is even talk of going for container loads of fish from Wick, to be transferred at Aberdeen on to Freightliner workings.

Trainload traffic reaches as far north as Lairg, in the shape of the British Petroleum oil tank traffic to sidings there. Other than that freight workings are only significant south of Invergordon. Despite the closure of the smelter, BR continued to handle bulk alumina bound for Fort William until 1984 and there is some whisky traffic from Invergordon Distillery. North Sea oil and gas industries in the Invergordon area generated trainloads of cement for concreting marine pipe in the early 1970s, and more recently, loads of pipe were conveyed from Hartlepool to be coated at Invergordon. North Sea oil platform yards are unfortunately not served by rail and transhipment of traffic is hardly attractive. Had the Government backed the proposals for a North Sea gas gathering pipeline, Nigg would have been the coastal base, with the chance of some business for rail.

Scenic splendour

The Kyle line's attractions are well-known, but nonetheless dramatic, and best seen — in the writer's opinion — on a bright September day with the Highland colours at their best. The sections that

Below:
Journey's end for the train at Kyle, with Skye across Loch Alsh. The 11.10 to Inverness waits behind Class 37 No 37.183 on 29 August 1983.
Neil Hargreaves

stand out for special comment include the climb west of Dingwall to Raven's Rock summit, with Strathpeffer nestling in the valley below, the first view of Loch Carron to the right of the train as it nears Strathcarron, and the dramatic approach to Kyle of Lochalsh (on a clear day, naturally) with the Cuillin Hills on Skye dominating a sparkling seascape. Not that the Wick/Thurso trains have much less to offer. Again, late summer/early autumn brings a striking range of scenic colours — blues, purples and browns — from the Dornoch Firth and the surrounding hills. From Helmsdale, the feeling is of the railway about to embark upon a heroic trek and indeed it does. Near the summit of County March, the isolation of the train in roadless country is breathtaking, particularly when a veiled sun highlights the foreground heather and grass while the Caithness mountains — huge, purple-grey shapes — rise in the distance above the bleak landscape. But, railwaymen in the Far North tend to be more philosophical, as a result of hard experience. Commenting on the scenic beauties when footplating a Class 37 locomotive to Wick one day, the Inspector accompanying the writer drily riposted: 'When you've played about in the snow', he said, 'the scenery loses its attractions'.

Top
Part of the Far North line that may be by-passed by the cut-off across the Dornoch Firth: the Kyle of Sutherland is crossed near Invershin by the 11.35 Inverness-Wick/Thurso of 10 August 1984. Class 37 No 37.260 *Radio Highland's* **train includes some Mk 2 stock.** *D. M. May*

Right:
Container handling facilities in Wick goods yard, in August 1984. *D. M. May*

Highland line versus A9

James Abbott

07.10 on a Monday morning in November 1984. Passengers queue for tickets for the London train: a commonplace phenomenon in the Southern suburbs, but in the Highlands of Scotland? For these passengers in the bright modernised concourse at Inverness will be joining the 07.20 'Highland Chieftain' IC125 service to London King's Cross, a train introduced into the timetable last May. Meanwhile, the 06.16 from Elgin draws in, two coaches behind a Class 37, and a score or so make the cross-platform connection to the 'Chieftain'.

This was the scene that confronted me before I wandered up the platform to the head of the London-bound IC125 (two power cars and eight trailers) and made myself known to Inspector Bruce of Inverness, who in turn introduced me to the man who would take us south, Driver Campbell, also of Inverness. With the semaphore signal controlling our road pulled off we were ready for an on-time departure. Since the trip was made, the resignalling scheme for Inverness has been approved. The guard buzzed up the right away; Campbell returned the signal, selected forward gear on the reverser, gave a double blast on the horn and opened up the throttle. 4,500 Paxman Valenta horsepower purred contentedly behind our backs as we edged out of the station, at 20mph maximum over the switch and crossing work in the station throat. The Aberdeen line dipped away to our right and underneath us as we passed

Above:
IC125 set on the Highland main line: the northbound 'Highland Chieftain' from King's Cross forges towards Carrbridge on 18 July 1984.
Mrs Mary Boocock

a yellow board bearing the legend 'HST 65' and Campbell opened up the throttle as wide as it would go. In a moment, though, he was throttling back: a red warning light on the console was indicating wheelslip problems. We were passing through a wooded stretch of lineside and the autumn leaf fall had rendered the rails greasy. The Valenta engines would have throttled back automatically when encountering wheelslip, but drivers are advised to make adjustment manually. When we were clear of the trees the red light went out and Driver Campbell opened up again for the run south.

The 'Chieftain' — a winner

Introduction of IC125 working to the Highlands in summer 1984 was seen by BR as a way of giving the area a better service by utilising spare time in the High Speed Train fleet. It was originally thought that the 'Highland Chieftain' would relieve the summertime load on the other daytime Inverness-London train, the West Coast-routed 'Clansman', but the 'Chieftain' has turned out to be a major success in its own right and has now been introduced to the timetable the

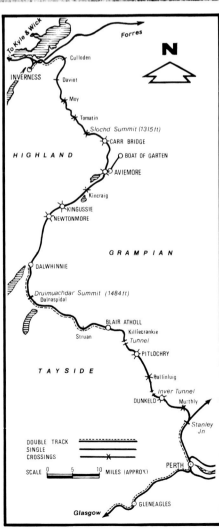

14

Left:
Resignalling at Inverness is in progress and will end scenes with semaphore signals like this. The 12.30 to Glasgow Queen Street passes Welsh's Bridge box on 27 April 1984. Motive power is Class 47/4 No 47.460 with snowplough fitting.
Mick Howarth

year-round. Not only has a through day train to destinations on the eastern side of England proved attractive, but the new possibility of a day trip to Edinburgh has generated much traffic. With an 07.20 departure it is possible for Inverness people to attend meetings in the Scottish capital starting at around 11 o'clock, have a working lunch and afternoon, and then take the down 'Chieftain' (departing Edinburgh 17.06) for an arrival in their hometown at 20.50.

The 'Chieftain' has a double-edged benefit: not only does it give Highland passengers a better service, but it also gives BR some useful resource savings. More effective use of train miles is achieved with the rerouteing of the 'Clansman' on summer weekends from May 1985.

The 'Clansman' is routed via Birmingham and its prime purpose is to provide a service from Scotland to the West Midlands, while falling in with the Wolverhampton-Euston half-hourly pattern. Scottish passengers can arrive in London earlier by changing into a train routed via the Trent Valley, so the London destination is not of central importance; an alternative service to London from the Highland line is now provided by the 'Chieftain'. Thus from the May 1985 timetable the 'Clansman' stock has been used to help relieve overloading of trains from Birmingham to the West Country on summer Friday nights. The stock lays over in Birmingham for a few hours on Friday evening, so the 'Clansman' is advertised as terminating at New Street — but on Saturdays the balancing working will be advertised as a Paignton-Inverness through service. On other days in summer, the 'Clansman' continues to work to London, but will terminate at Birmingham in winter.

The A9 — as viewed from the railway

The 'Highland Chieftain' pushed on south through Culloden, past a siding holding tar tanks with bitumen for the roads and on to the first single-track section. The turnout from double track to single track here is to be upgraded to give a faster running potential for HSTs — this is part of a package of improvements announced recently for the Highland line. Over Culloden Viaduct, built to take two tracks but now accommodating just one, and on to Daviot, end of the double track section going south in Highland Railway days.

Left:
In the pass of Killiecrankie, the 13.35 Glasgow Queen Street-Inverness is powered by a Class 47/4 on 25 August 1984. *W. A. Sharman*

And so to Moy, with the schedule comfortably in hand as we passed signal AM366 (signal controlled from *Aviemore* box at Moy) at 07.39.

The signal indicated line clear ahead and the advanced warning system mechanism gave aural affirmation of this. During the journey there was a regular high-pitched 'peeping' — a reminder of the presence of another safety aid, the driver's vigilance device. Formerly known as the dead man's handle, the vigilance device on an HST power car comes in the form not of a handle but a pedal which has to be depressed once a minute by the driver in response to the peeping.

As we ran over the wooden trestle bridge prior to the passing place at Moy itself, Inspector Bruce pointed out of the cab to the left: there on the hillside was a huge 'M' etched in the trees, in honour of Mackintosh, laird of Moy.

Now there was evidence of the major investment going ahead in the main road running parallel to the Highland main line, the A9, with widened formations and unweathered concrete structures. It is the massive amounts of public money that have been lavished on the A9 (£237million is being spent on it between Perth and the Cromarty Firth) that have given BR so many headaches with the Highland line in recent years. The main problem has been

that since 'deregulation' of long-distance coaches under the 1980 Transport Act, coach operators have been able to fully exploit the improved infrastructure of the A9 (without paying a penny extra for the improvements — public service vehicle licence fees are often less than those for a private car), while ScotRail has to compete with a tortuous 19th century alignment, any improvement of which must be paid for out of BR's own funds.

With the improvements to the A9 coach operators found that they could offer transit times on the Glasgow/Edinburgh-Inverness routes that were competitive with rail. With capacities of around 50 passengers per vehicle, the coach companies found they were able to get a good payload from the main cities and were

able to offer cheap fares and cut out intermediate stops, thus further bettering end-to-end transit times by comparison with rail. In addition, improvements in vehicle comfort standards won more passengers for the coaches. Thus there was an inversion of the pre-1980 position, where BR had been the long-distance carrier and road operators had provided local services, to one where the coaches were cleaning up on the trunk moneyspin-

Above:
The River Spey valley near Kingussie: Class 37 No 37.029 heads an Inverness-Edinburgh Millerhill air-braked freight train on 13 June 1984.
A. O. Wynn

Right:
Between Slochd and Carrbridge comes the 16.30 Inverness-Edinburgh Waverley behind Class 47/4 No 47.431 on 21 April 1984. *D. M. May*

Above:
Class 47/0 No 47.206 comes off the impressive Culloden Moor viaduct on 12 August 1982 with the 14.30 Inverness-Glasgow Queen Street.
W. A. Sharman

Left:
The 10.20 Sundays Inverness-King's Cross IC125 of 19 August 1984 approaches Dunkeld, in Strath Tay. *Michael McGowan*

ners and leaving the trains the sweepings at the wayside stations.

It is easy to appreciate that the financial consequences of all this were dire, and in 1983 matters were so grim that ScotRail had to decide whether to fight the coaches on price or forsake the business for good. At the time, a Glasgow/Edinburgh-Inverness single on the coaches was £5, while by rail the same journey cost £11.70. Although BR hoped to generate some traffic by cutting prices, there was no way that loadings would more than double in order to maintain total revenue and although BR was ever-vigilant on the cost front, cost cutting could not make up the shortfall either. But something had to be done, or the entire railway system north of Perth was in danger of falling like a house of cards. Unlike the coach operators, BR has a social obligation to maintain a service to local communities — in recognition of this, the Government pays BR Public Service Obligation grant. The Government has made it plain to BR that the PSO grant should be cut, so there was no succour for the Highland line there. Without the

Above:
Aviemore's hotel facilities appear in this view of the 09.22 Edinburgh Waverley-Inverness behind a Class 47 on 24 July 1982. *S. Rickard*

long-distance revenue and with falling PSO support the sums were coming out wrong. It was with this backdrop that BR had to decide whether to adopt a policy that would adversely affect total revenue in the short term, or allow coaches to become fixed in the passengers' minds as the obvious mode. There was no choice. ScotRail took the offensive.

A strategy had to be evolved that would minimise the revenue loss, and here BR played the coach boys at their own game. An extra train was put on when loadings were heaviest, northwards on Friday afternoons, matching the coaches on price (£5) for Glasgow-Inverness journeys, but the usual fare to intermediate stops. This may have seemed inequitable to passengers from the wayside stations, but there may be some justification for ScotRail's argument that these communities should have been thankful for the maintenance of a public transport service. The 'Jacobite', as the train was called, showed the travelling public that BR was still very much in the market. Passengers still perceived BR to be the better bet on speed and comfort (even though with the latest models of coaches that may no longer be the case in actuality), and those that had

deserted rail on price grounds returned. The 'Jacobite' was kept for the 1984 season (but from Edinburgh rather than Glasgow and with the price upped to £6), and was one of the first trains to offer video entertainment. The more positive marketing of the Highland line exemplified by the introduction of the 'Jacobite' proved the turning point of the rising against the coaches. Some of the smaller coach operators have been experiencing difficulties, and this has eased BR's task, although the road ahead should not be thought by any means easy.

Up to Slochd

In the days of steam, enginemen would have said that the road to the top of Slochd Summit should not be thought by any means easy, with long stretches at 1 in 60: but matters seem somewhat different from the head end of 4,500 diesel-powered brake horsepower. We eased up the grade at 65mph — we could have gone at 75mph if necessary, but there was plenty of time in hand. Over the top and through a rock cutting to have a fine moorland scene laid before our eyes — if somewhat marred by the scarring A9. We were slowed to 60mph on an engineering slack for a new bridge going in a week later to take a curve out of the road as the secondman (who had worked in on the Elgin turn and would normally have been occupying my seat) emerged with a brew-up.

Into Aviemore, where we were feathered into the up platform — normal practice, I was informed, is for the 'Chieftain' to use the down platform to save passengers a trudge over the bridge, but on the day I travelled the down 'Royal Highlander' was running late and we passed at Aviemore rather than Slochd.

At Aviemore a sharp blast of Highland air greeted us as a former driver, now a guard's inspector, opened the cab door (HST cabs are air-conditioned and slightly pressurised to keep any engine fumes out) and swung up. '116 on leaving Inverness', he informed us, and a further 45-50 passengers joined at Aviemore: satisfying loadings for November on a line where the seasonal imbalance in loadings is of the order of 8:1. But it wasn't the gratifying level of patronage that this former 'Black Five' driver had come to tell us about: no, it was to see if this diesel really could do what in his driving days would have been thought laughable, a 'ton' on the Highland line.

For the day I travelled on the 'Highland Chieftain', 12 November 1984, was the day that the line speed was raised south of Aviemore to include a stretch at 100mph. A light-hearted debate ensued about the merits of the different types of traction — the diesel men asserting that the HST would soon be reaching Perth in two hours or less while the steam man talked of the cab of a 'Five' at 80mph ('those speedos were never accurate' was the retort). Euan Cameron, ScotRail Passenger Business Manager, told me later that a 2hr timing is a target for 1986-7, and although it would be technically feasible, BR still had to decide whether or not it was worth it, as the necessary track and signalling improvements might prove expensive.

We passed another HST speed differential board — up to 90mph now. The boards allowing a raise of speed are square, while those bringing HSTs back to line speed (marked 'HST T') are diamond-shaped — so a driver with route knowledge will be able to judge when he may go faster, even when the boards are covered with snow, Bruce commented. The inspector explained that differential speeds for HSTs are possible because the units have superior braking characteristics — and they are kinder to the track.

Now 100mph was authorised by the lineside board, and we streaked through the moorland scenery in the front of the first fare-paying passengers on the Highland line to travel at 100mph. In the smooth-riding cab of the HST there seemed little difference as the needle nudged three figures, except for the high spirits of the BR men. The stretch authorised for 100mph is 2¼miles long, from MP74 to MP76¼, and there are 90mph stretches on either side, giving a worthwhile spell of fast running.

Deceleration for Kingussie, third pick-up point for the 'Highland Chieftain', where a further score joined the train. As soon as all were aboard we headed off south again, through Newtonmore where the loop is soon to come out in order to increase through running speeds. Down to 65mph for a wooden bridge just outside Newtonmore — there is little that can be done about this restriction. Now we were on the 16mile drag up to Druimuachdar Summit (1,484ft) — from here to Blair is the section most badly affected by the worst of the winter weather.

There was intermittent flange contact on the sharp curves on the climb, but Bruce said there is much less with the HST than with Class 47 locomotives. The power equipment is distributed over two

vehicles each weighing 70t rather than one weighing 100t, and the traction motors are not axle-hung as with other BR locomotives, but mounted on the bogies: thus the passage of an IC125 exerts less wear on the permanent way.

At Dalwhinnie we passed the second down London sleeper, waiting to gain the single-track section we had just left. In the reorganisation of sleeper services that took place in October 1984, seating accommodation was added to the 'Royal Highlander', which had previously been sleeper only: now both London-Inverness sleeper trains carry seated passengers. On the Anglo-Scottish sleepers generally, BR has lost business due to shorter daytime train transits and more frequent air services. The long Inverness route has suffered less from these factors than the route to lowland Scotland.

Over Druimuachdar

Over the summit we were on another double-track section. One feature here is that there are two successive intermediate block signals (distinguished by a white rectangular plate with vertical stripe affixed to the mast). Thus it is possible to have three trains on this part of the route at any one time — but the up line is controlled from Dalwhinnie, and the down line from Blair, so signalpost telephones on either side of the line send off messages in different directions!

Down from the summit on a favourable 1 in 70 grade, through Blair Atholl and back on to single track. Blair is one of a number of Highland communities aggrieved that the 'Highland Chieftain' rushes through non-stop. The up train never has stopped here, but the down one did prior to the October 1984 timetable changes. ScotRail has decreed that both London daytime trains, the 'Highland Chieftain' and the 'Clansman', will stop only at Aviemore, Kingussie and Pitlochry between Inverness and Perth. The local authorities of the areas affected were up in arms, but BR stood firm: it says it needs the up to 13min improvement in end-to-end timings that the limited number of stops gives as a valuable

weapon in its battle with the coaches.

Killiecrankie Tunnel: the severest restriction on the Highland road. Speed is kept below 30mph due to the sharp curves in the tunnel, and as we emerged we travelled over the viaduct with the river foaming to our right. The flanges squealed as Driver Campbell notched the accelerator up to wide open to take us up to line speed of 60mph outside the tunnel.

At Pitlochry Campbell positioned power car No 43043 well forward from the platform so that the TGS vehicle at the rear would be correctly placed for loading of mails. About 20 passengers joined and we were away again punctually, only to be held further up the line at Dunkeld. The signal was pulled off for the down line and the crew were wondering what it might be. Some 8min later the answer was provided in the form of a DMU converted for use as a sanding machine, which had been covering the line to assist with the autumnal conditions.

Now the 'Highland Chieftain' was coming out of the Highlands and moorland scenery had been replaced by rolling farmland with the occasional pheasant hopping over the rails in our path. Arrival in Perth at 09.35 was 7min behind time as a result of our wait for the sanding machine. At Perth I disembarked, as did the Inverness men, handing over the 'Chieftain' to a Haymarket crew. For me, it was a comfortable ride through lowland Scotland 'on the cushions'. For the Highland line to my back the ride ahead in the battle with the A9 looks far from comfortable — but the outlook is much less bleak than it was two years ago. Initiatives such as the 'Highland Chieftain' show that BR is not battle-weary but charged with adrenalin. May the best mode win.

Below:
Highland dew at Dalwhinnie on 28 July 1984. The 07.06 Edinburgh Waverley-Inverness has Class 47/0 No 47.013. *W. A. Sharman*

North by northeast — Aberdeen-Inverness

Elgin West signalbox, with ScotRail liveried Class 47/7 No 47.711 *Greyfriars Bobby* accelerating with the Sunday 09.25 Glasgow Queen Street-Aberdeen-Inverness on 10 March 1985. The leading coach is a Mk 1 micro-buffet, but the rest of the train is a strengthened push-pull set. The return Inverness-Aberdeen-Glasgow Queen Street train in the afternoon has been so well patronised that a 19.05 Inverness-Aberdeen relief has been run, also a 19.00 from Aberdeen-Inverness. *Philip J. Wylie*

Michael Harris

NOWADAYS, Table 240 in the BR passenger timetable looks prosaic enough with its neat pattern of trains over the Aberdeen-Elgin-Inverness line which belies the onetime complexity of railway services in the area. Fortunately, this has been a case where rationalisation of facilities has paid off and the route seems capable of further development, too. The Aberdeen-Inverness service is effectively a bridge between the West Coast and East Coast main lines, with connections to be made each way from Elgin and Keith into/out of north and southbound long-distance services at Inverness and Aberdeen. As noted in the introduction, Aberdeen-Inverness fits into the ScotRail InterCity service grouping along with Edinburgh-Glasgow, Aberdeen-Edinburgh and Aberdeen-Glasgow which perhaps indicates its bias towards the East Coast route.

First to Inverness

In fact, a railway line first reached Inverness *from* Aberdeen, when the route through Keith and Elgin was completed in 1858. Once trains from Perth came to Inverness via Forres, the role of the Aberdeen line as a north-south link changed. Two railways were involved, with the Highland Railway and Great North of Scotland combining to provide a through rail connection between Aberdeen and Inverness. However, the Highland Railway tended to regard the section from Forres to Elgin and Keith as a branch to its main line south to Aviemore and Perth. For its part, the GNSR expended more effort in building up traffic from Speyside and the Moray Firth ports to feed through Aberdeen. Nonetheless, apart from throughout journeys made possible by connections between HR and GNSR trains at Keith, there were Aberdeen-Inverness workings with the engines of either company taking trains through from 1908. There were three routes beyond the now closed Cairnie Junction: the GNSR's Speyside line through Craigellachie, that Company's coast route serving Portessie and Buckie, and, beyond Keith, the HR line from Keith Junction through Orbliston to Elgin. A union between the GNSR and HR was proposed, but did not materialise in the years before World War 1, although one positive result was the operation of faster through trains between Aberdeen and Inverness.

Retraction

After Grouping, competition from road services led to the thinning out of services, or their withdrawal from some branches, but there was little in the way

Above:
The 13.40 Aberdeen-Inverness near Inveramsay, northwest of Inverurie on 2 April 1985. The motive power is Class 47/4 No 47.546. *D. M. May*

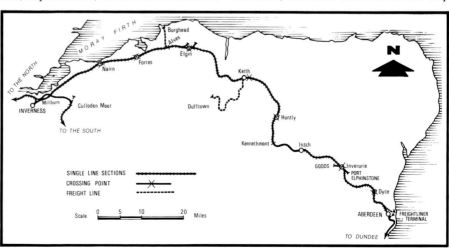

SINGLE LINE SECTIONS ┼┼┼┼┼┼┼
CROSSING POINT ━━✕━━
FREIGHT LINE ┄┄┄┄

Scale 0 5 10 20 Miles

of overall rationalisation until the 1950s. In 1954, there was a general recasting of passenger services in northeast Scotland, including the rerouteing of Aberdeen-Inverness trains over the former HR line via Mulben, with a commensurate improvement in through timings. In July 1960 came two InterCity DMU services each way between Inverness and Aberdeen, taking 2½hr for the 108 mile journey with four intermediate stops.

Another pair of workings soon followed, and the DMUs were notable for their buffet service. Before long, implementation of the Beeching Plan brought with it wholesale rationalisation to the area, in time leading to the closure of most intermediate stations between Aberdeen and Inverness, singling of the line and the abolition of numerous signalboxes and loops. Not only that, but the Speyside route lost its passenger service, as did the

Above:
A strengthened Mk 2/Mk 3 push-pull set in its former livery, in the River Don valley near Dyce, forms the diverted 09.05 Glasgow Queen Street-Inverness of 13 May 1984 with Class 47/7 No 47.707 *Holyrood* at its head. *D. M. May*

Below:
The River Spey viaduct can be seen in the middle distance as a loaded grain train for Elgin disturbs the peace on 2 June 1983, powered by Class 47/0 No 47.082. Larger capacity wagons now convey most of this traffic. *M. M. Hughes*

Dyce-Fraserburgh line while the coastal line was largely closed to all traffic. So by the late 1960s, northeast Scotland boasted only the Inverness-Aberdeen passenger service, worked by the Class 120 DMUs which covered half a dozen trains each way to an overall 2½hr timing; these called at the remaining seven intermediate stations. Meanwhile, wagonload freight traffic continued to decline.

The late 1970s

After a decade of little change, the late-1970s heralded several developments, including refurbishment of the DMUs from 1977. In May 1978, the offshore oil boom was having its effect on Aberdeen and the North Sea coast, and the resulting housing development suggested a potential for a cross-city passenger service, introduced between Stonehaven and Inverurie. The experiment was short-lived and the through trains were withdrawn later in 1978. The innovation had encouraged hopes of restoration of the Aberdeen-Fraserburgh passenger service but, during 1979, BR announced that the freight-only line beyond Dyce was slated for closure. Despite the oil boom, only one freight service each way remained to Fraserburgh. True, there was potential, but the condition of the track meant that £1million would be needed to bring it up to a standard to handle existing business, and no less than £3million investment for upgrading of Dyce-Fraserburgh to handle high-capacity wagons for rail to gain the chemical traffic generated by coastal development. Money was not available from BR's own resources and, with no contribution forthcoming from local

Above:
High capacity grain wagons for the Scottish Malt Distillers works at Roseisle on the freight-only Burghead branch approach the former Coltfield platform behind Class 27 No 27.008 on 31 August 1984. *Rod Muncey*

authorities, Dyce-Fraserburgh closed completely in October 1979. Elsewhere, the new industrial developments in the Moray Firth were generally served satisfactorily by sea, and the staple freight traffic on rail was generated by the whisky distilleries. For this, the Keith-Dufftown and Burghead lines remained open. Incoming grain benefited by investment in privately owned wagons while a container crane at Elgin had been installed to handle Freightliner traffic.

Below:
Freightliner containers, moved by passenger trains from Aberdeen-Inverness-Wick, are seen at the head of the 13.45 Aberdeen-Inverness, hauled by Class 47/0 No 47.209 on 19 September 1984. The train is approaching Keith.
Paul A. Biggs

Loco-hauled services

Despite earlier refurbishment, the Class 120 DMUs were soon to be transferred from Scotland, and loco-hauled sets were introduced on the Aberdeen-Inverness trains from 10 March 1980, retaining the buffet facilities that had been a feature of the DMUs, and with the overall journey time reduced to 2hr 22min. The new signalling centre at Aberdeen, commissioned in January 1982, brought with it the control of the Inverness line as far as Dyce. At the other end of the route, the new Inverness signalling centre will in time control as far as Elgin. Another development in the early 1980s was the introduction of Sunday trains, including the re-routeing of the morning Glasgow-Inverness, and return afternoon train to run via Dundee-Aberdeen and Elgin. The Class 47 motive power on these trains was matched on the Aberdeen-Inverness workings as well. The five-car second-class only sets used for the basic timetable currently feature early Mk 2

Left:
A bulk grain trainload working from Burghead leaves Keith (with Strathisla distillery's whisky barrels stored in the distance) on 31 May 1983 with Class 47/0 No 47.093 as motive power.
M. M. Hughes

Below:
The reopened Dyce station has been a great success, and on 21 March 1985 provides a few passengers for the 10.32 from Inverness headed by Class 47/0 No 47.117. *D. M. May*

steam-heated, vacuum-braked stock. In the absence of Class 47s, a pair of Class 26s normally substitute at the front end.

Road competition

The 1980s have so far seen a number of developments on the Aberdeen-Inverness trains. The deregulation of the bus and coach industry tempted a private operator to run an Aberdeen-Inverness service, but appropriate reponse from Scot-Rail, and the far from satisfactory timings possible on the through A96 road, contributed to withdrawal of the competition during 1982. Traffic on the Inverness-Aberdeen line far exceeds that of other northern routes, with 732,000 passenger journeys recorded in 1984.

With the May 1984 timetable, the Inverness-Aberdeen trains were retimed to provide better connections at the Granite City into and out of Glasgow trains while another innovation was the 05.52 Elgin-Aberdeen, to go forward from Aberdeen via Edinburgh, Birmingham and Bristol as a through train to Penzance. Then, on 15 September 1984, came the reopening of Dyce station, a notable example of a combined ScotRail/local authority initiative. Apart from calls by Inverness trains, there are three Aberdeen-Dyce workings each way. From the start, Dyce generated encouraging business and, by the spring of 1985, forecasts indicated that almost 180,000 journeys will have been made in the first year, over 150% above the target of 70,000 originally expected. However, ScotRail is ready to acknowledge that the success of Dyce will doubtless attract competition from bus

operators in the wake of forthcoming deregulation of the industry. Another success has come with the connection provided by the 06.16 Elgin-Inverness into the 'Highland Chieftain' IC125 service. Early starts are necessary for travellers bound for the south and England in view of the long distances involved — Elgin is 200 miles from Edinburgh, and 600 from London. It is a measure of the reduction in journey times made possible by IC125 services that Elgin-King's Cross via Inverness takes 9hr 44min, and 9min less using the 05.49 to Aberdeen. The 08.00/10.00 King's Cross-Aberdeen IC125s give a 9hr 13min overall journey time to Elgin by connections into the 15.40/17.40 Inverness trains from Aberdeen. The RAF bases in northeast Scotland contribute to the carryings of the Inverness-Aberdeen trains which also are reasonably busy with parcels traffic.

As to freight business, the current decline in the market for whisky has naturally affected Speedlink traffic. The most positive recent development has been the loaded containers from Aberdeen-Inverness-Wick conveyed on passenger services. These have been somewhat sporadic, but their introduction was significant in overcoming the hurdle of conveying loaded freight by passenger train. Extension of the principle could lead to container loads of fish similarly conveyed from northeast Scotland to Aberdeen for the south.

Scenic potential

Although perhaps lacking the grandeur of some other Scottish railways, Aberdeen-

Above:
The 'Northern Belle' cruise train from Aberdeen-Keith-Dufftown and return was introduced in 1984. On 29 August of that year, Class 47/4 No 47.410 shunts the stock of the 'Belle' past Dufftown platform towards the goods yard before the return working. *Rod Muncey*

Inverness has some particularly attractive stretches, notably in Strath Bogie and between Keith and Elgin and the view from the carriage window provides vistas over the Moray Firth and across to the Black Isle during the approach to Inverness. The scenic potential of the line has seldom been realised to the full, until the enterprise of Grampian Railtours, with wholehearted support from ScotRail, saw the introduction of the 'Northern Belle' in May 1984. Using first-class stock from a 'Nightrider' working, with restaurant car, the 'Belle' leaves Aberdeen in the mid-morning for Keith Junction, calling at Dyce and Inverurie. The 'Belle' then takes the freight-only Dufftown branch (formerly the GNSR route to Elgin and Speyside). Lunch is served during a stop at an attractive location on the branch. At Dufftown, there is an escorted tour of the Glenfiddich Distillery, and an optional visit to Drummuir Castle. After rejoining the train, afternoon tea is served. Aberdeen is regained at 18.25. In 1984, 4,000 passengers patronised the 'Belle' and, for 1985, the season has been extended with 32 advertised workings between mid-May and September. The 'Belle' is also available for private charters.

For the future, the loco-hauled Aberdeen-Inverness workings are expected to be supplanted by Class 150 DMUs.

East Coast interlude: Aberdeen-Edinburgh

The East Coast route from Berwick-on-Tweed through Edinburgh, and across the Forth and Tay bridges, is frequently in sight of the sea, and highly scenic it is, too.

Left:
The collapse of Penmanshiel Tunnel meant an enforced diversion of the ECML, to the south of Dunbar. The 12.15 Edinburgh-King's Cross IC125 is just south of the former tunnel on 10 June 1981. *T. H. Noble*

Below:
The mighty Forth Bridge is being crossed by the 09.45 Edinburgh-Aberdeen on 29 January 1981, behind a Class 47/4. *Brian Morrison*

Above right:
Class 27 No 27.023 takes the 12.21 Dundee-Edinburgh away from the Tay Bridge on 5 March 1983. *D. M. May*

Centre right:
A tranquil scene at Broughty Ferry, east of Dundee, on 5 February 1983 with the 10.30 Aberdeen-King's Cross IC125 making its mark. *D. M. May*

Bottom right:
Railway enthusiasts keep a watch out for the southbound West Coast Postal, the 15.45 Aberdeen-Carstairs, here approaching Arbroath on 25 March 1985 behind Class 47/4 No 47.562 *Sir William Burrell.* *D. M. May*

Above:
ScotRail livery for the first three vehicles of the 15.30 Aberdeen-Edinburgh Waverley of 7 April 1985. Class 47/7 No 47.705 *Lothian* is propelling near Inverkeilor.   *D. M. May*

Right:
New livery, too, adorns this IC125 set forming the 08.00 King's Cross-Aberdeen on 4 April 1985, near Drumlithie, south of Stonehaven.   *D. M. May*

Below:
Freight for Aberdeen hurries north near Portlethen, on the coast south of the Granite City and where the station reopened in May 1985. The locomotive is Class 47/0 No 47.108, and the date, 3 April 1985.   *D. M. May*

South of Perth : Perth-Stirling

The Stirling-Perth line is surely one of the finest stretches on ScotRail's trunk routes, but less often regarded as a scenic attraction. It also sees a variety of train working.

Above:
The Fair City of Perth looks particularly so on 28 July 1984 as the 13.25 Glasgow Queen Street-Aberdeen crosses the River Tay behind Class 47/4 No 47.418. *W. A. Sharman*

Below:
A perfect setting surrounds the 15.06 Edinburgh Waverley-Perth headed by Class 47/4 No 47.414 on 4 July 1984, and seen near Gleneagles. *D. M. May*

Above:
A handsome ScotRail liveried ensemble makes up a Glasgow Queen Street-Perth excursion en route to the city's Railfair on 13 April 1985. The push-pull stock with Class 47/7 No 47.708 *Waverley*, seen near Forteviot, in Strathearn was one of several star attractions. *D. M. May*

Below:
Also near Forteviot is the southbound 'Highland Chieftain' IC125 — 13 April 1985. *D. M. May*

The West Highland line – a line for all seasons

Michael Harris

IT IS a little sobering to realise that the West Highland line will not see the centenary of its opening until 1994, for it was in August 1894 that 10 chains less than 100 miles of new, single-track railway (the West Highland Railway, a separate company, operated by the North British Railway) were ceremonially opened between Craigendoran and Fort William. The same year saw the passing of the Act for the Mallaig Extension, nearly 42 miles of line that, concrete viaducts and all, did not open until 1 April 1901. These 150 miles of railway, so patiently fought for and laboriously built, nearly fell victim to the Beeching Plan. It is a matter of history that they didn't, and the rationalisation of the 1960s effectively added another arm to the West Highland. The former Callander & Oban line, once under the aegis of the rival Caledonian Railway, was cut short at Crianlarich in the autumn of 1965, and

Glasgow-Oban trains have henceforth used West Highland metals from the Clyde to Crianlarich.

Escaped they might have done from the jaws of closure, but the combined 180 route miles of the Glasgow-Crianlarich-Oban/Fort William-Mallaig lines saw little overall promotion until the early 1980s. True, there had been dieselisation, and long-distance timber traffic won to feed the now-closed Corpach pulp-mill, but a traveller on the West Highland line in the early-1970s would not have seen much evidence to ensure that Britain's most outstanding *group* of scenic railway routes would make the West Highland Railway's centenary. One turning point was the compelling British Rail film of 1981, *A line for all seasons*, which surely fired a whole range of influences to bend their energies to promoting greater use of the West Highland.

If 1983 saw initiatives, the next year saw consolidation, show business even,

with the operation of steam hauled excursions on the Mallaig Extension. The 1985 season should see further burnishing of the image, as far as tourist traffic is involved, and the introduction of timetabled Sunday trains over the whole of the West Highland network for the first time in its history.

Incentive for action

Competition from road services has had the effect of stimulating a more competitive approach and, as with the Glasgow/Edinburgh-Inverness and Inverness-Wick coach services, at least one private operator has entered the market for Glasgow-Fort William traffic, although

Below:
The Caledonian Canal locks at Banavie, on the Mallaig line. The 06.50 from Mallaig is arriving at Banavie station on 26 July 1984, behind Class 37 No 37.081 *Loch Long*. *W. A. Sharman*

Left:
Tourist routes in the summer maybe, but in winter the Highland railways are frequently the only lifeline. The Oban line has more 'indigenous' traffic than the West Highland proper, being catered for on 18 January 1985 by (top) the 13.00 Oban-Glasgow Queen Street with Class 37 No 37.033 and (bottom) the midday train from Glasgow with No 37.112. Both trains were photographed in Glen Orchy, between Dalmally and Tyndrum Lower.
Both: Ray Anthony

trains and distributed questionnaires to elicit passengers' views. The results from the survey confirmed that the vast majority on these Mallaig excursions were visitors in the area with their cars. Special attractions were offered on trips such as an optional sea cruise and a Highland piper. Overall, the programme of Sunday trains was profitable, and was extended in operation in 1984 to run on 11 Sundays.

Sunday excursion trains returned to the southern part of the West Highland line, too, in the shape of Edinburgh-Oban workings during July and August 1983. Some of these stopped at Westerton en route from/to Cowlairs for Glasgow area passengers. A Glasgow-Edinburgh Mk 3/Mk 2 air-conditioned push-pull set was used, with *ETHEL 1* providing electric power to the train headed by a Class 37. The excursions incidentally offered a means of running road tests with the new conversion. After the first two trains, subsequent trips were sold out, and ScotRail was particularly pleased at what was seen as a new way to combat the excursion road coach market. Hostesses were provided on these excursions, West Highland line souvenirs were on sale and announcements over the public address system were also in French and German. The Edinburgh-Oban Sunday trains had 100% loadings in 1984 and summer 1985 sees a summer Sunday Glasgow-Oban train, too.

Sunday excursion trains on the West Highland line are nothing new, and workings to Fort William and beyond started in the 1930s. Such trains, to Fort William only, recommenced in 1949, but were withdrawn in 1957 during an economy drive.

With trains to Oban and from Fort William to Mallaig in 1983, there remained only the Crianlarich-Mallaig Junction section without regular Sunday services. Only four signalboxes have to be opened between these points for through traffic, and May 1985 saw the introduction of a Sunday evening Fort William-Glasgow Queen Street train with sleeping cars from Euston and a 17.20 Glasgow-Fort William. Sunday mornings and afternoons are needed for engineering work north of Crianlarich, but, even so, mystery excursions may be run to Fort William.

primarily in the summer season. It is worth remembering that the (mostly) 50mph maximum line limit of the West Highland line means that Skye-Ways Coaches 3hr Glasgow-Fort William timing has ¾hr in hand as compared with the rail schedules, as well as providing a Sunday service. Even so, the more energetic approach from ScotRail in 1983, says Chris Green, General Manager, ScotRail, saw the Highland Regional Council and the Highland & Islands Development Board take a more positive interest in BR's developments.

The fine weather of summer 1983, some fares incentives and the operation of various excursions boosted West Highland line passenger receipts by 25% as compared with 1982. The improvement looks less impressive when the previous summer's industrial stoppages are recalled, but traffic on the West Highland line picked up immediately the strikes were over, so the number of days' services completely lost was small; indeed some trains ran part of the way during the dispute.

Colin Shearer, the then Area Manager, now succeeded by Clive Evans, was the inspiration for the trains run on four Sundays in August 1983 between Fort William and Mallaig. Two return trips were made, going out at 10.30 and 14.15 from Fort William. The trains were marketed locally at a special £3.50 fare as a way of getting holidaymakers out of their cars and on to rail to do their sightseeing and on average 200 passengers were carried on each of the return trips. A BR supervisor travelled on the

Catering for the tourists

The observation saloons between Fort William and Mallaig have proved a notable success, with double the passengers carried in 1983 as compared with each of the 1981 and 1982 seasons. In all, the facility attracted 3,600 passengers and surveys showed that 20% of custom would not have considered taking the train in the absence of the saloons. For 1985, there are more developments. LMS-design, BR-owned ex-inspection saloon No 45030 will be the observation car between Glasgow and Oban (reintroduced in 1984) and LNER-design inspection saloon No 1998 *Loch Eil* (owned by Steamtown) will be used between Fort William and Mallaig. For the Fort William-Mallaig steam workings, Fort William has been allocated a set of Mk 1 coaches, with refurbished interiors and with public address fitted, which have been painted at Eastfield in the cream and green livery used by the LNER in the 1930s. A buffet service is available. Steam reappeared on the Mallaig Extension in May 1984 and that summer saw over 11,000 journeys made on the steam excursions, representing a 20% boost to summer passenger travel on the line; charter trains were also operated. The steam service is now treated as a business in its own right, using 'marginal' resources and initially ScotRail is committing itself to a three-year programme. For 1985, steam operations have been extended to an out and back service five days a week (Sundays-Thursdays inclusive) from 17 June-8 September, with spring bank holiday services, too. The Mallaig Extension also has the addition of a new station, at Loch Eil, near Fort William, to serve the Outward Bound centre. This was constructed by the centre under ScotRail supervision and was opened to traffic in May 1985.

For 1985, a Class 101 DMU has been painted in Scottish Tourist Board colours to operate an Oban-Crianlarich service, with a bus connection from Fort William. The tourist DMU will serve Loch Awe station, reopened in May 1985, and provide a link with the steam boat operating on Loch Awe. The third leg of the circular tour takes passengers back to Fort William by service train from Crianlarich.

Lochaber District Council has been working closely with public transport operators to develop tourist package holidays in the area, based on Fort William and Inverness as centres. Hoseasons Holiday offers cruising 'self-drive' holidays on the Caledonian Canal and Loch Ness. The brochures encourage intending holidaymakers to use the Mallaig line and bookings are accompanied by the inducement of a voucher offering a 50% reduction in the cost of the ordinary return rail fare to the Highlands. For 1984, the Scottish Tourist Board publicised an extension of these package holidays. In 1983, circular tours based on Oban, involving a bus connection to Fort

Above:
One of the specialities of the West Highland Railway was — and mostly still is — its handsome chalet stations with their island platforms. Steam heating is another less enviable distinction, and apparently still needed on 23 June 1984! The station is Tyndrum Upper, and the train, the 14.15 Fort William-Glasgow Queen Street, one of the pair of passenger services introduced in October 1983.
Nigel Hunt

William, thence by rail to Crianlarich and back to Oban, attracted about 10/15 round-trippers on peak days and, in 1984, the recently introduced 14.15 train from Fort William made possible a more ambitious Oban-Fort William-Mallaig-Crianlarich-Oban round trip, as a result of the better timings available. Indeed, the circular trips became possible only in 1983 as a result of a minor retiming at Crianlarich, in which the 5min later running of the 18.23 Glasgow Queen Street-Oban allowed it to provide a connection out of the 18.22 ex-Fort William. For 1985, the tourist DMU will make its appearance.

The tourist potential of the Highland railways has been recognised all too slowly by those involved, but the availability of the HIDB's Travelpass, not to

speak of Britrail passes held by overseas visitors, means that 20% of all Highland lines (not only the West Highland) passenger traffic nowadays is made up of card-toting travellers.

As to the balance of traffic on the West Highland lines, the Glasgow-Oban service has a higher level of indigenous travel with 166,700 passenger journeys recorded in 1984, as against the total of 167,500 for

Glasgow-Fort William; each figure, it should be remarked, is below the passenger traffic volume of Inverness-Wick/Thurso. The balance on the Fort William and Oban lines is roughly 50/50 indigenous and summer tourist traffic.

Improved timetabled services

Although the May 1983 timetable was shown as lasting the full year, from 3 October 1983 there were a number of significant changes to West Highland passenger services, bringing them into the basic interval timetable that is now a standard feature of ScotRail timetables. On the Oban line, the midday train was advanced to a 12.20 Glasgow departure from 12.55 so as to give an official connection at Oban into the last Calmac sailing for Craignure and Mull, and likewise the 17.58 train from Oban was slightly retimed to give a better boat connection. The 08.00 Oban-Glasgow was accelerated by 15min in running time compared with the former 07.40. These alterations were accompanied by changes in crew workings for Oban men, and the introduction of self-contained stock diagrams for this line; previously the train sets covered Fort William, Oban line and Glasgow-Dundee trains.

The West Highland line proper saw a major development from the same date with the introduction of a convenient morning train at 09.50 from Glasgow Queen Street throughout the year, on Mondays, Fridays and Saturdays only in winter and every weekday from June-September, returning similarly from Fort William at 14.15. As Archie Roberts, Transport Officer for Highland Regional Council, comments: 'This was something that my Council had been seeking for years'. Not only did this give most parts of Scotland the chance for connections into a convenient morning departure — as compared with the 05.50 from Queen Street which conveys the London sleeping cars, or the former 08.34 'dated' summer train — but it opened up the market for day excursions from Glasgow and central Scotland to Fort William and even to Mallaig — the latter with a 10min turn round!

The existing trains were also significantly altered from October 1983, with the morning 08.40 from Fort William (previously 09.19) reaching Glasgow 43min earlier, and the 17.40 (previously 18.22) from Fort William into the Scottish metropolis at 21.42, instead of 22.28, at the same time providing a reasonable connection to Edinburgh to arrive at 23.00.

The only through Mallaig-Glasgow working is by the 15.50 from Mallaig, this train being formed of air-braked stock which in part constituted the other major development of the October 1983 changes — the introduction of Mk 3 sleeping cars between Euston and Fort William. These are accompanied by Mk 2 air-conditioned seating vehicles which work to Mallaig and back.

There was every chance in 1983 that with the withdrawal of Mk 1 sleeping cars, Lochaber would have been deprived of its overnight London service. Had this happened, the 06.00 Glasgow-Fort William would have been retimed to 08.30. Adverse public reaction to the possible withdrawal of facilities persuaded the operators to seek a solution and the initiative of the Scottish Region's locomotive engineers resulted in the emergence of *ETHEL* — electric train heating

Left:
Few passenger trains in the UK convey fuel oil tankers, but that's the way Mallaig-based trawlers receive their fuel by rail. Empty wagons are returning on the 06.50 Mallaig-Fort William, headed by Class 37 No 37.188, seen arriving at Glenfinnan on 12 June 1984. *A. O. Wynn*

Facing page,
The West Highland line has seen increasing freight traffic in the last few years, a vital development to ensure the future of this spectacular route. The general freight trains are Class '7', as illustrated in these two pictures.

Top:
The morning train from Mossend yard, near Glasgow is alongside Loch Treig, between Corrour and Tulloch on 17 August 1984. At the front end is a Class 37.

Bottom:
Just leaving one of the typical West Highland viaducts, in this case just north of Rannoch, is the early morning down freight from Mossend-Fort William, headed by Class 37 No 37.151 on 20 August 1984. The trees are to the east side of lonely Rannoch station. *Both: M. M. Hughes*

ex-locomotive. The problem of the West Highland line was that its Class 37 motive power was equipped for steam heating only. For a cost of £3,000 or so each, three Class 25 diesel locomotives were converted at Aberdeen Ferryhill depot to serve as generator 'vehicles' to provide electric power to Mk 3 sleeping cars and Mk 2 coaches.

The Fort William sleeping cars now run with the Euston-Inverness 'Royal Highlander' in both directions throughout the year, so that the famed title now applies to the Fort William section for the first time.

As mentioned earlier, from May 1985 a Sunday timetabled service has been introduced between Fort William and Glasgow. On Saturdays, the 15.50 from Mallaig-Glasgow Queen Street has accommodation for seated passengers only, but provides a facility into a sleeping car service from Glasgow Central to the south. The sleeping cars at Fort William are held over to the Sunday evening, to work south to Euston, arriving Monday morning.

The use of the *ETHELs* will be fairly short-lived, as the programme for fitting electric train heating equipment to a batch of Class 37s is now in hand and the first Class 37/4 as these will be known, should appear shortly.

Freight developments

It was expected that as a consequence of the industrial disputes of 1982 freight traffic on the West Highland line would be lost and indeed one of the three Mossend-Fort William and return freight services was suspended. However, with the resumption of normal working it was necessary to run specials to clear the available traffic and by mid-1983 the third pair of trains was restored; in January 1984 these were designated as Class 6 company trains, conveying alumina from Blyth to Mallaig Junction

outward and returning as empties. At present, there are three Class '7' trains each way, two down, and one up to/from Corpach. The West Highland line generates about £2million of revenue for Railfreight annually, roughly divided 50-50 for incoming and originating traffic. The two main industries are paper manufacture at Corpach, alongside Loch Eil on the Mallaig line, and the British Aluminium Company's plant at Fort William. The closure of the pulp mill at Corpach in 1980, supplied with timber loaded to rail at Crianlarich Lower yard, reduced the previous freight trains five each way to three. But there is still talk of the establishment of a new pulp mill at Corpach, although if realised it would take three years or so to become operational. Paper making at Corpach requires china clay, which is worked up on Speedlink services from Cornwall and conveyed on the midday Mossend-Corpach air-braked freight. Outgoing paper is dispatched on the midday train to Mossend, and Speedlink offers a next-day arrival in southeast London. Rail brings in 85% of the Corpach mill's input — the greater part, of course, being wood pulp.

Aluminium ingots and products from the BAC plant are dispatched on the 06.01 Fort William-Mossend. Other new traffic includes timber from Arrochar, Fort William and Taynuilt to Welshpool and Hereford with timber loaded from Loch Treig forest between Tulloch and Corrour (there is no road access) to rail on one train a week to Fort William. Another recent traffic flow comprises barytes from Carstairs to Fort William, for Strontian.

Coal class traffic ceased to be worked to Oban, Crianlarich and other West Highland line stations from November 1983 and consignments to the whole area are now distributed by road from Mossend. Officially, Oban freight depot is closed but some wagons, mostly loaded with

fertiliser, will probably be handled there for the time being. The rest of the Oban line's freight movements comprise three trainloads a week of oil to British Petroleum at Connel Ferry and to BP and Esso at Oban. Oil moves in wagonloads for industrial purposes to Fort William and Corpach, and once a week to the trawler fuel depot at Mallaig. In the last case, the tank wagons are conveyed at the rear of the 16.05 Fort William-Mallaig passenger train. Other miscellaneous consignments include a healthy business in high-class shellfish by passenger train, loaded at Fort William on to the overnight London train, and a variety of Red Star parcels.

Resources

The opportunities for a reduction in operating costs are, as already noted, dependent on investment in new equipment. The total staff complement for the lines north of Arrochar is 250-300, of which just over half are operating personnel. As to reductions in operating costs, the abolition of steam heating on passenger trains would eliminate double manning.

Another major change would involve the replacement of existing signalling by radio electric block token, first introduced on the Kyle line. The earliest that REBT could be contemplated on the West Highland would be mid-1986, and the cost of the scheme is put at over £1million. REBT would enable the line to be opened for specials at any hour or any day at minimal cost and would result in a 'captive' locomotive fleet which would be dedicated to West Highland line operations. At present, there is tokenless block signalling between Crianlarich and Rannoch, introduced in 1967. Electric token working operates over the following sections: Craigendoran-Crianlarich, Rannoch-Mallaig Junction. Fort William station is signalled from a panel in

Mallaig Junction box, with colour light signals. On the Mallaig line there is one-train working from Mallaig to Glenfinnan, and electric token operates Glenfinnan-Mallaig Junction. Banavie level crossing was renewed in 1983, and the associated signalling replaced using finance from the European Economic Community Regional Development Fund. On the Oban line, Oban itself has no signalbox and there is 'no signalman' key token working Taynuilt-Oban, and electric token operates Taynuilt-Dalmally and Dalmally-Crianlarich.

The condition of the way and works of the West Highland line gives no particular reason for concern, although there is a considerable mileage of bullhead rail and wooden-sleepered track, and the introduction of the Class 37s has increased the track maintenance required. Unlike the Inverness-Wick/Thurso line, there is little chance of improving alignments to increase the line speed limit above the prevailing 50mph. The Mallaig line has even fiercer restrictions, with a 30mph limit Mallaig-Glenfinnan Viaduct, 25mph over the viaduct and 40mph to Banavie.

The buildings and structures on all lines are in good order, with the exception of Oban station, the overall roof of which is unsafe — passenger trains use the adjoining platform to the structure. The BR Property Board's first proposal for redevelopment of the station was turned down by the local authority last year, but a new scheme has been submitted. The revised proposal for redevelopment was the subject of a public inquiry in March 1985. This would provide for a new station behind the buffer-stops of the present working platforms, and also

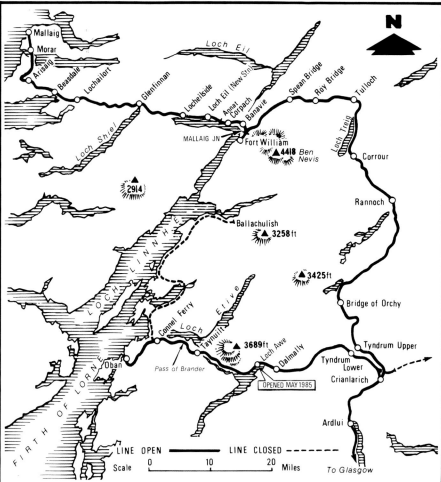

Above:
In the left background is the Loch Laggan dam, and on the morning of 15 July 1983 trains have just crossed at Tulloch station in Glen Spean. Nearest is the then 06.00 ex-Glasgow Queen Street with Class 37 No 37.178. *M. M. Hughes*

include housing development. Planning approval has been granted, but progress is dependent on the consent to demolish a listed building as the concourse and overall roof of the existing station are 'listed'. Fort William station was resited and new buildings provided in 1975. Of the West Highland Railway's original and distinctive stations, most have survived reasonably well intact, although Arrochar and Ardlui have suffered from subsidence. One major alteration at a number of stations is the provision of powerful lighting. Except for the lack of its footbridge, the structures at Rannoch remain almost exactly as built.

Apart from the through London service, West Highland line passenger trains are formed of Mk 1 stock whose condition has been the subject of complaint, on the grounds that although these services may not be under the InterCity banner, with journey times of 3-4hr the customer is entitled to higher standards. Certainly, the 1950s-vintage Mk 1s cut a poor figure alongside modern road coaches. The need to retain steam heating on the West Highland line for the present limits the choice of vehicles, while the drive to rid the coaching stock fleet of coaches insulated with blue asbestos has compounded the operator's difficulties. From 1977-82, the Region upgraded its fleet of Mk 1 open seconds with renewal of the moquette, table surfaces and linoleum, only to lose them in 1981-2 in the course of a campaign to withdraw vehicles insulated with asbestos. They were replaced by older steam-heated TSOs free of asbestos from other Regions, but as classified repairs are not being given to steam-hauled Mk 1s if better replacements can be found, the ScotRail allocation as currently deployed on the West Highland line is far from settled and consequently the vehicles are admitted as being variable in their standard of decor. There are only eight dual-heated TSOs (Tourist Second Opens) on Scottish internal services, but these (and SKs [Second Corridors] used other than on the West Highland line) have been face-lifted with flourescent lighting, painted vestibule ends and carpets provided in aisles and compartments. From 24 January 1983, other than on the Fort William-London workings, accommodation on West Highland line services has been second-class only.

Catering is an important element for the West Highland trains although the financial results are poor. Miniature buffet facilities are provided in BSO(T) (Brake Second Open-buffet facility) and TSO(T) vehicles on all Glasgow-Fort William workings, generally south of Rannoch or Tyndrum where the attendant switches from northbound to southbound trains, but throughout on the 09.50 down and 14.15 up trains. From May 1984, the Oban trains have had catering facilities during the summer only, with a trolley service from/to Glasgow. An attempt to continue train catering into the winter proved a commercial failure.

Local support

Speaking to David Blair, Chief Executive of Lochaber District Council, he stressed the Council's view that public support for the West Highland line should not be under-rated: 'The line is part of Lochaber's heritage', was the comment.

Most vulnerable of the Highland lines has seemed to be the Fort William-Mallaig section, with its minimal local (as opposed to through) passenger traffic. Concerned at the need to ensure the line's survival, at the Mallaig end there is a strong lobby from the Road to the Isles Marketing Group to ensure the continuing development of the Mallaig extension for tourist traffic. The introduction of the steam workings in 1984 owed much to the efforts of the Group and to the Transport

sub-Committee of the Morar, Arisaig and Mallaig Community Councils. The latter, in particular, is pressing for the establishment of a railway and fishing industry museum at Mallaig. All concerned feel that even more should be done towards national promotion of the Mallaig line's attractions and, in particular, some want to see Mallaig added to the list of Golden Rail resorts.

The latest development in public lobbying is the creation of the Friends of the West Highland Line, a pressure group based in Glasgow which seeks to promote the fortunes of the Oban and Fort William/Mallaig routes, and public meetings have been held in Glasgow, Oban, Morar and Fort William. Details of the organisation may be obtained by sending a stamped addressed envelope to 56 Turnberry Road, Partick Hill, Glasgow G11 5AP.

Long-term prospects

Increased freight traffic on the West Highland line depends on the success of Government agencies in their efforts to re-establish a pulp mill at Corpach, to be fed by Highland spruce, much of which could be delivered by rail. Similarly, the Scottish Development Office is regarded as a very positive force by BR in endeavours to secure new flows of freight traffic to rail, in particular felled timber.

Tourism could see further expansion by investment in new facilities, in particular with Lochaber District Council's scheme for a major sports centre near Fort William station, and the same authority's ambitious proposals for a major multi-

million pound ski centre to be created on the slopes of Ben Nevis, providing finance can be attracted from EEC sources.

But the essential attraction lies in the railway routes themselves, and the unrivalled vantage points from the trains of West Highland scenery. Its beauties have been portrayed in BR's attractive film *A Line for all Seasons* and the Area Business Group is relaunching the *Line for all Seasons* brochure, now available in three languages.

The grandeur of the West Highland lines is best conveyed by photographs, and brochures are available which provide a step by step route guide to the routes. Tranquil and alluring the lines may appear to the summer tourist, but it can be a different matter in winter. Severe weather in January 1984 saw the West Highland blocked by snow north of Crianlarich. After the 14.15 from Fort William was stopped at Tyndrum Upper during the afternoon of 21 January, the line was closed to passenger traffic north of Crianlarich to Fort William until 06.00 on 27 January.

Although locomotive-hauled passenger workings will remain in the immediate future, Class 150 DMUs are the prospect before long — providing they prove themselves suitable for the lines. Perhaps thought could be given to the development of a 'customised' observation version of the Class 150 which would enable passengers to enjoy to the full the marvels of the West Highland line, in the approach to the centenary of its construction.

Right:
An LMS-design inspection saloon, serving as an observation car, brings up the rear of the midday Mallaig-Fort William train, approaching Locheilside on 14 June 1984 behind Class 37 No 37.264. *A. O. Wynn*

Steam to Mallaig

Steam locomotives gave way to diesel traction on most of the Highland railways in the 1960-62 period, and few believed they would reappear. But steam attracts the tourists, and from May 1984 there have been summer steam workings between Fort William and Mallaig and more feature in the 1985 programme.

Left:
The real star in 1984 was a former North British 'C' 0-6-0 No 673 *Maude*, owned by the Scottish Railway Preservation Society; these engines were staple West Highland motive power in years past. *Maude* heads a charter train, seen at Banavie outward-bound from Fort William on 28 May. *Tim Grimshaw*

Below:
Maude was seriously taxed by the Mallaig route, and on this occasion it worked this special train to/from Arisaig only. The 0-6-0 makes a fine sight as it crosses Loch Nan Uamh viaduct, on the outward run. *J. H. Cooper-Smith*

Right:
The Mallaig Extension featured concrete viaducts, the most spectacular of which is at Glenfinnan, with its dramatic view down Loch Shiel. Nicely posed is LMS '5' 4-6-0 No 44767 *George Stephenson* (these engines were latter-day steam power on the West Highland) en route for Mallaig on 11 July 1984. *W. A. Sharman*

Bottom right:
No 44767, again, this time seen shortly after leaving Lochailort for Mallaig with one of the 'regular' steam turns. 11 July 1984. *W. A. Sharman*

Far right bottom:
The third steam locomotive used in 1984 was another '5', No 5407. On 28 May, it fights for adhesion on 1 in 50 gradient to Glenfinnan station, with the 11.10 Fort William-Mallaig. *David Eatwell*

Making the best of the Sou'west: Carlisle to Glasgow and Ayr to Stranraer

Michael Harris

THE essential pre-Grouping characteristics of our railways will not be erased, in all probability. In Scotland, certainly, old rivalries and economic influences of a century and more are reflected in much of the surviving network. After Grouping, the dominance of the Caledonian over its erstwhile rival, the Glasgow & South Western Railway, was ensured within the London Midland & Scottish Railway's administration. The Sou'West generally came second-best to the Caley inheritance in terms of the provision of new rolling stock and facilities. Under BR's Modernisation Plan, the Glasgow-Ayrshire Coast-Stranraer workings were covered by diesel multiple-unit schemes, and improved services introduced, but the Sou'West's Glasgow-Kilmarnock-Dumfries-Carlisle line saw a continuing decline in prestige. Its principal role, that of an alternative route to the Caley main line over Beattock, was emphasised when the progress of electrification north of Weaver Junction in the early 1970s resulted in the regular diversion of West Coast main line services. By then, its own through passenger express trains were largely residual and, as a result of Beeching rationalisation, freight services were sparse. Although the Beeching Plan had originally cast some doubt on the survival of any rail access to Stranraer, economies were realised by the complete closure of the 'Port Road' from Dumfries-Newton Stewart-Challoch Junction in 1965. Thereafter, services to and from Stranraer and the south had an enforced long march via Ayr, Mauchline and along the Nith Valley line. The future was unclear, for it was even possible that this was merely an interim step before further, more drastic closures.

Retrenchment, then suspended animation

After 1965, the picture presented was somewhat discouraging and there were no apparent plans for investment in either the Glasgow-Dumfries-Gretna Junction section or south of Ayr. A downgraded main line was linked by a very secondary route west of Mauchline to a single-line railway south of Ayr, largely untouched from pre-Grouping days and generating minimal intermediate traffic and comparatively little through business. To handle diverted West Coast main line express services during electrification, some speed restrictions along the Nith Valley line were eased, but the Carlisle resignalling brought with it singling between Gretna Junction and Annan while Barrhead to Kilmarnock was similarly treated before 1974. Electrification saw one London-Glasgow and return daytime InterCity train routed over the Sou'West main line, in addition to an overnight Euston-Glasgow sleeping car train and the Euston-Ayr-Stranraer 'Northern Irishman'. No real changes occurred on the DMU-worked Glasgow-Ayr-Stranraer service

and the two routes settled into a period of suspended animation, overlaid with feelings of an uncertain future. The only real opportunity had been glimpsed with what proved to be unrealised plans for Hunterston's deep-water port. These had included proposals for coal and iron ore to be worked south over the Sou'West via Annbank and Mauchline en route to Redcar.

The Northern Ireland effect

Outside influences began to have their effect with the decline of existing England-Northern Ireland shipping routes from Liverpool, Preston and Heysham, such that Stranraer-Larne was clearly destined to become the only significant service across the Irish Sea to the Six Counties. Much of the growth had been taken up by roll-on/roll-off road freight, but the market expanded to offer opportunities to rail, helped by the unsatisfactory nature of road access to Stranraer by the A75 west of Dumfries. Political and economic implications arising from the entry of the UK and Eire into the European Economic Community also have had some effect in enhancing the status of the Stranraer-Larne link which is served by two shipping lines — Sealink and Townsend Thoresen, the latter operating out of Cairnryan, but not directly rail-served.

This dynamic of increasing business through Stranraer, naturally influenced to some degree by Northern Ireland's particular political and social climate, was beginning to impinge on the railway network, faced with its own set of problems: an absence of policies for the commercial development of the Sou'West lines, a need to come to terms with imminent engineering renewals on the Nith Valley route and an urgent requirement to seek replacements for DMUs working from Glasgow to the Ayrshire Coast. Management remained too decentralised at area level such that the set of problems spread across several concerns. There were Area Managers at Dumfries and Ayr and a Shipping and Port

Left:
Annan station on 5 September 1983, with a Class 107 DMU forming the 11.37 Dumfries-Carlisle. *J. Checkley*

Manager at Stranraer. From January 1981, the Dumfries and Ayr areas were merged and, exactly three years later, the Area Manager, Ayr took responsibility for ScotRail matters at Stranraer Harbour. The picture emerges of the opportunity created to make better sense of the Sou'West network by virtue of more powerful management emanating from Ayr. In the meantime, the approval in 1983 for electrification of the Paisley-Ayr/Kilwinning-Ardrossan lines dealt with the need to modernise the Ayrshire Coast services. The two remaining areas for improvement were by now clearly delineated: a review began in 1982 of the future for the Nith Valley route and a working group, led by operators, was set up to consider the future improvement of the Ayr-Girvan-Stranraer line. To lapse into the vernacular, ScotRail was getting its act together to tackle a backlog of indifference and engineering obsolescence, let alone commercial opportunities, in the southwest of its territory.

The Nith Valley route

The Sou'West's 107-mile main line from Gretna Junction to Glasgow is one of the underrated British railway engineering achievements, epitomised by the 181ft masonry span of Ballochmyle viaduct, near Cumnock. There are no gradients of note for the first 38 miles out of Carlisle, and then, five miles beyond Dumfries, begins the climb at 1 in 150/200 to Drumlanrig Tunnel. Beyond, the railway runs along a beautiful stretch of Nithsdale, before the ascent into the Ayrshire uplands. There is then the 17-mile descent to Kilmarnock, and thereafter sharp climbs for north and southbound trains between there and Glasgow. Restrictions around curves in the Nith Valley and elsewhere limit overall speed. The most obvious characteristic is the

paucity of intermediate traffic between Dumfries and Kilmarnock, with the decline in the wagonload business and closure of small stations. With the prospect and then authorisation of electrification of the Caley main line, the Nith Valley route was maintained for the diversion of Anglo-Scottish traffic. Thereafter, the singling south of Annan and between Barrhead and Kilmarnock limited its capacity for through main line working. The objective then was to keep

the route going, and no more: standard civil engineering renewals but no investment.

The traffic offering along the route could not justify investment to keep the

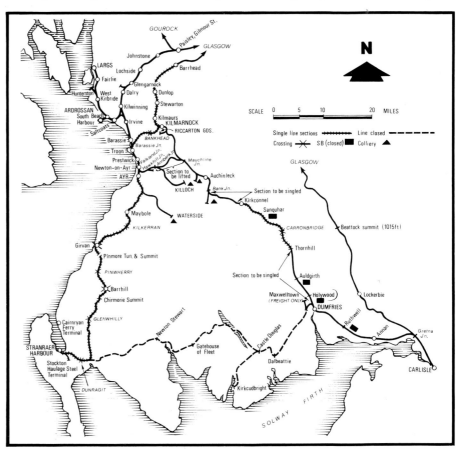

Two views taken in the Drumlanrig Gorge, where the 1983 freight train derailment resulted in single line working between Kirkconnel and Thornhill, although the up line remained largely in situ.

Left:
A Carlisle-bound air-braked freight train is hauled by Class 47/4 No 47.541 *The Queen Mother* on 30 April 1984.

Below left:
The wooded slopes of the valley are seen at their best as the 12.40 Carlisle-Glasgow Central of 2 May 1984 is the charge of Class 27 No 27.010.
Both: M. M. Hughes

track would prejudice the rationalisation proposals, and the short-term solution was to single between Thornhill and Kirkconnel (nearly 15½ miles) as the intermediate crossovers at Carronbridge were unsuitable for regular working. Lengthy sections of the former up line nevertheless remained in situ. The timetable then in force assumed double track operation, and so the unwanted intervention provided a practical demonstration of partial singling on the line. As a result of experience the investment submission was reworked.

The Nith Valley route's rationalisation scheme will start later this year, for completion during 1986. The breakdown of the £4million project divides 50/50 into track and signalling. Double track will extend from Kilmarnock to Bank Junction (to Knockshinnoch opencast coal site) then single track to south of Holywood with passing loops (similar in design to those on the Highland main line, eg Kincraig) at Kirkconnel and Thornhill. The turnouts will allow trains to maintain full line speed on the through line. The reuse of the displaced second track will minimise the provision of new materials. Associated with the scheme is the closure of the line between Mauchline-Annbank used from 1965-75 by through trains to/from Ayr and the south, but currently with a north-facing junction only at Mauchline. Through traffic to/from Ayr is now worked over the Kilmarnock-Barassie line. This latter line is not included in the rationalisation plan but it is to be upgraded to allow 60mph running, while an automatic half barrier installation is planned at Gatehead to replace existing manned barriers. From May 198- the line has been controlled from Barassie box; in due course it will come under Paisley signalling centre.

The Nith Valley line will in future be worked under track circuited block, the most suitable solution for a long, single line, with control from signalboxes at Annan, Dumfries (northwards to New Cumnock) and Kilmarnock. In the process the gate crossing at Holywood will be replaced by AHBs.

Dumfries and other stations

Despite its decline as a railway centre from the mid-1960s, Dumfries retained many of its former facilities until a rationalisation scheme in 1982. This saw closure of the traincrew depot, with reallocation of its work to Ayr and

downgraded main line as a double track artery. Also the mechanical signalling, in some cases still reliant on pre-Grouping equipment, was in urgent need of replacement. Viewed in 1982, by the end of 1984 11% of the double track would need renewal, and by the end of 1986 50% would have to be replaced. With the route's operating ratio of 403% it was clear that resources needed to be slimmed to suit the traffic offering.

At first sight, ScotRail could either contemplate piecemeal reductions in facilities as renewals became necessary — effectively the 'do nothing' option — or complete closure; or there could be rationalisation with investment. Closure had to take note of the fact that the West Coast main line did not have the capacity to handle the Sou'West trains and, even if it did, journey times would be unacceptably lengthened. Further, the Nith Valley line had a crucial role as a diversionary route, particularly as it is seldom affected by snowdrifts, as was proved in January 1984 when the West Coast line was

blocked. Also, the Caley main line was known to face extended engineering work, involving ballast cleaning and the premature renewal of continuous welded rail, a programme that will last until 1987. Rationalisation with investment was clearly the preferred option for the Nith Valley line.

£4million investment

The 74 miles of double track between Kilmarnock and Annan were, therefore, proposed for investment involving major rationalisation. Outright singling was out of the question, as the entry points to the double track were (and remain) single lines: south of Barrhead, from Barassie, and from Gretna Junction. The submission to the British Railways Board was for the singling of four 15-mile sections, with almost 12 miles of double track between New Cumnock and Mauchline. Before action could be taken, a derailment in July 1983 saw ¾ mile of track destroyed between Carronbridge and Kirkconnel. Reinstatement of double

Left:
A past scene at Barassie Junction, where the Troon avoiding line diverges. Class 47/4 No 47.469 is working the 13.15 Stranraer Harbour-Euston on 11 September 1981. *Les Bertram*

Kilmarnock sees improvements

The large station at Kilmarnock, in line with that at Dumfries, experienced declining fortunes after the Beeching closures. Into the early 1980s, the town had only six main line trains each way daily, and yet was continuously staffed for the infrequent service. The picture has greatly changed with the introduction of the improved Passenger Transport Executive supported DMU service, while an innovation began in 1983 with experimental Kilmarnock-Ayr workings on summer Saturdays and on Kilmarnock Fair days. These trains were extended to daily operation from June-September in 1984, with through cheap fares and connections from as far south as Annan. This initiative by the Area Manager Ayr was welcomed by local staff who distributed mail shots. Success in 1984 has been followed by a three trains each way service this summer, for the first time advertised in the BR timetable. Kilmarnock station is due to be refurbished shortly.

Freight is limited

The majority of freight traffic over the Nith Valley route is for Stranraer and shipment, and otherwise is limited to the ICI works at Dumfries and near the Ayrshire coast, oil to Maxwelltown and Dumfries and Ministry of Defence movements to Annan and near Dumfries. The main development on the main line northwards has been at Knockshinnoch, near New Cumnock, an opencast coal mining site that includes a washery. The line from Bank Junction has been refurbished by BR, and traffic was due to start by rail when the National Union of Mineworkers dispute intervened; sub-

Carlisle and a reduction in station staffing. In addition, some main line signalboxes such as Ruthwell, Auldgirth and Sanquhar were closed. This scheme reflected the low originating revenue at Dumfries, but the proposed cuts caused public disquiet at a time when plans for general rationalisation of the main line were in the air. It was also clear that low revenue was a result of a commercially unattractive passenger service, and poor connections at Carlisle. From May 1983, the existing through trains were supplemented by DMUs running to/from Carlisle, effectively giving Dumfries a two-hourly service to the south. The result was a significant increase in traffic, aided by the introduction of Saver tickets, such that some train loads were soon revealed as 90% better than in 1981.

Dumfries has since seen further improvements, not least a £200,000 plan involving modernisation of the station's passenger facilities and its road approach recognised by an award in the Association of Railway Preservation Societies Best Restored Station Competition of 1984). Concern regarding possible closure of the main line brought with it greater involvement in rail services by Dumfries and Galloway Regional Council. With only five stations in the whole of its area the Council had previously evinced little interest in the Nith Valley line which was regarded as a strategic link rather than as a local amenity. Improved working relations between ScotRail and the Council resulted in the issue of Senior Citizen concessionary fares and a Scot-Rail card. Closer rapport between Scot-Rail and the Council then engendered the establishment of the Galloway Bus Link in October 1983. This joint enterprise between ScotRail, the Council and bus operator (Western Scottish), in marketing an integrated bus/rail timetable, provides for through ticketing from former rail-served towns such as Newton Stewart, Kirkcudbright and Castle Douglas with a reasonable range of specially designated bus services timed to work into/out of Dumfries station. Results so far have been reasonably encouraging although the prospect of reorganisation of the bus

industry has inhibited further development of the Bus Link.

North of Dumfries to Kilmarnock, the withdrawal of stopping passenger services during the Beeching era saw the closure of all intermediate stations, although, for no very clear reason, Kirkconnel was eventually retained. In the wake of the Dumfries rationalisation, this station, previously continuously manned, was intended to become unstaffed. Local reaction to this bid was vociferous and eventually effective in securing the retention of single shift manning; the controversy that had arisen had the benefit of stimulating increased use of the station. If Kirkconnel could generate over £40,000 passenger revenue annually, the 6,000 population of Auchinleck ought to do better. This town is just within Strathclyde Regional Council's jurisdiction, and a decision was made in November 1983 to build a new station almost on the site of the old. The joint venture between BR and Strathclyde saw a £190,000 station opened on the former station site in May 1984. Farther north, Kilmaurs station was opened from the same date, benefiting from an hourly off-peak Kilmarnock-Glasgow introduced with the 1984-5 timetable. The only other possible candidate for reopening north of Dumfries is Thornhill, although the railway is one mile from the village.

Below:
A fortnight before the reopening of Auchinleck station, in May 1984, this view reveals the new platforms, footbridge relocated from the now-closed Crookston station, and original stone station building left of centre. *Les Nixon*

sequent movements were by road. Killoc Colliery will in future be served from Annbank and the west only. Kilmarnoc has suffered from the recession, and th only whisky traffic on rail is in ferr wagons to the Continent. Riccarton (to th south of the town) receives a once-week block oil working from Grangemouth.

Glasgow-Carlisle passenger traffic

The remnants of the former Midland G&SW Anglo-Scottish trains disappeare with the withdrawal of the Glasgow Nottingham via Settle & Carlisle working in May 1982. The service current consists of an overnight sleeping car trai from Euston-Glasgow making intermed ate stops on the G&SW main line, th Euston-Stranraer sleeper each way, an the more recently introduced Eusto Stranraer day train. This had develope from a Carlisle-Stranraer summer trai first introduced in the late 1970s. Thes are supplemented by Carlisle-Glasgo semi-fast workings, four each way, and daytime weekend Euston-Glasgo service.

Ayr

The biggest single change to the area railways is naturally the forthcomin electrification from Paisley to Ayr, an Kilwinning to Ardrossan, together wit resignalling and general modernisatior The £80million project will cost about 9 less than originally forecast, thanks t new technology, in particular affectin lineside electrification equipment (les relay rooms are required) and signalling Originally programmed for completion i May 1987, the introduction of electri services from Glasgow to Ayr will nov come in October 1986; Ardrossan will sti have to wait until the next year fo electrification. The resignalling wi result in the replacement of 36 mech anical signalboxes by an extension to th existing Paisley Gilmour Street signallin centre.

Electrification is vital to a revival of th fortunes of the Ayr-Glasgow service which have suffered at the hands of fierc competition for commuter traffic, as consequence of deregulation in the bu industry. The same effect has als savaged carryings from/to Largs, still th

subject of discussions between BR and Strathclyde PTE as to possible electrification beyond Ardrossan. In the meantime, ScotRail is hard put to maintain acceptable service quality, given the ageing fleet of Class 107 DMUs. For the premium commuter traffic, from May 1984 the set for the up 'Royal Scot' has travelled out from Glasgow at 06.00 to cover the 07.55 from Ayr (so also giving an additional London service) and 'Nightrider' stock is used for the 17.12 ex-Glasgow Central and 18.45 return. These and other moves initially brought back commuters to rail, but in the past year general coach competition has become stiffer, and so taken more business from BR. Associated with electrification are developments at Ayr, including modernisation of the station facilities and completion of the Townhead carriage cleaning depot which will in due course service the electric multiple-units based at Corkerhill.

In the meantime, there have been improvements in freight facilities at Ayr, with the rationalisation of Falkland sectioning sidings. However, the plan for a new coal concentration depot at this location met with stiff resistance from coal merchants unwilling to move from their old facilities. Even before the NUM dispute, coal traffic in Ayrshire was greatly reduced as compared with the 1960/1970s, and the one major originating point is Waterside, on the former Dalmellington branch. This is an opencast site, with coal production managed by a contractor. Traffic began moving again by rail shortly after NUM members returned to work.

Ayr probably now has a better regular long-distance passenger service than at anytime in its history; before 1965, there was neither a daytime nor overnight through train to London, the latter coming with the diversion of the 'Northern Irishman' after closure of the Dumfries-Stranraer line. The 21.00 sleeping car train from Euston is not only of value for passengers, but conveys newspapers and letter mails from London and Manchester. Ayr's parcels post travels to Glasgow by rail, but Scottish letter mails, such as to Edinburgh, now go by road.

The Stranraer Road

That greatly missed railway historian, the late David L. Smith, has left us with graphic descriptions of locomotive and train working south from Ayr to Stranraer. It is certainly one of the most difficult single line sections of railway on BR, in view of the severity of its gradients, and their location, curvature, and the exposed and bleak nature of an under-rated scenic route. The challenge starts at Ayr with the climb away from the station steepening to 1 in 70 to Dalrymple Junction then, after a downhill respite, there is another ascent, latterly at 1 in 75/80, to Maybole. Undulations follow to Girvan, where from the platform end there is the fearsome climb mostly at 1 in 54/56 to short of Pinmore Tunnel. The northbound approach from Pinwherry is more broken, but includes stretches at 1 in 65/69. Beyond Pinwherry, southbound trains face about eight miles of steady climbing mostly at 1 in 67/80 including some severe curvature. The descent from the summit at Chirmorie is more broken, but northbound trains face a three-mile climb at 1 in 57/58.

This 59-mile railway is now the rail link between Britain and Northern Ireland, and the growth of freight traffic over the line is all the more remarkable when considering the difficulties it presents for train operation. There was singling north of Girvan and west of the former Challoch Junction in the wake of Beeching, and the Ayr-Stranraer line has seen nothing in the way of investment until recently. It speaks volumes for the quality of local railwaymen that Stranraer has continued to be so well served by rail.

Improvements have begun with the strengthening of bridges south of Girvan, to raise the line to RA8 standard and allow a maximum axle weight of 22.9 tonnes; this work was completed by the end of 1984. Previously, there was a restriction on the use of some Class 47 locomotive variants (Class 47/7s are still prohibited), and freight wagons over 21.3 tonnes axleload. This improvement to bridges is the only major upgrading planned at present, but another bugbear, the passing loops' restriction to trains = 52 SLUs, will be reviewed for possible remedy in due course. However, as they become due for renewal, the turnouts at loops will be designed for 50mph running in place of the present 10mph. Signalling continues to be token working.

Section 8 success

Catalyst for freight traffic development over the Stranraer line was Scotland's first grant-aided facility under Section 8 of the 1974 Railways Act, opened by Peter Parker in October 1976. The rail freight terminal at Stranraer, on the main line east of the former Town station, was built and equipped by a road-haulage firm, Stockton Haulage Ltd. The company had been carrying freight by road for Northern Ireland and the Irish Republic for over 10 years, and in 1973 decided to transfer to rail steel carryings from northeast England to Stranraer for shipment. As traffic built up, Stockton Haulage opted to build a transhipment depot, with gantry crane and mobile equipment so that ferry traffic could be more easily transhipped; it travels on to the ferry on Stockton Haulage's road trailers. Soon after the opening of the terminal, BR introduced a Glasgow-Stranraer air-braked freight working to feed into the Speedlink network. Before the terminal was opened, rail freight carryings over the Ayr-Stranraer line totalled 20,000 tons annually, and the figure has climbed to today's 100,000 tons or so a year.

The success of Stockton Haulage's terminal led to an application for a further Section 8 grant, to triple capacity and impove facilities by providing two new sidings, vastly increased covered accommodation and additional cranes. The £400,000 extension to the terminal was officially opened by BRB Chairman, Bob Reid in November 1983. In addition to steel traffic, Stranraer is now handling fertiliser and cider, as well as a wide range of other business, some originating on the Continent.

In addition, there has been a huge increase in carryings of new cars for the Northern Ireland market. None were

Left:
Photographers, by and large, tend to neglect the Ayr-Stranraer line. This is Pinmore viaduct, south of Girvan on 25 April 1984, with Class 37 No 37.195 at the head of the evening Stranraer Harbour-Carlisle Speedlink train, mostly consisting of empty wagons. *Les Nixon*

Left:
Technicolour Sealink boat train: the 13.35 Stranraer-Glasgow Central, with its eye-catching repainted Mk 1 coaches, passes Elderslie, southwest of Paisley, on 26 May 1984 with Class 47 motive power. *Mrs Mary Boocock*

From the 1970s, the flow of passenger from Northern Ireland has changed con siderably. As a result of the 'Troubles people left Ulster but return frequently t visit friends and relations. Also, there ha been a growth in short break holidays t Britain which has similarly expanded th market.

As already noted, parcels (particularl mail order) and postal traffic betwee Britain and Ireland is considerable and i sponsored by the Director, Parcels BRI Apart from the overnight train fro Euston, there is also a parcels onl service, train No 1S40, the 05.15 Eustor Stranraer. This picks up vans from variety of originating points and convey sizeable consignments of traffic fro Britain to Northern Ireland and Eir Sealink provides the manpower at Strar raer Harbour, where post and parcels ar transshipped on to road trailers fc conveyance on the ferry. 1S40 is balance by train No 3M07, the 03.37 Stranraer Euston, which mainly carries parcel post; once again, there is an imbalance (business *to* Northern Ireland.

As a result of a £500,000 modernisatio scheme, completed in late June 198 Stranraer Harbour station now ha greatly improved facilities. To cater for passenger business of 300,000 passenge annually, a new station enclosure an covered walkway almost to the ship sid have been provided, and platform faci ities modernised.

Management effectiveness

The Sou'West at last looks like comin into its own, thanks to a more effectiv and imaginative approach by ScotRa management, largely the result of a wide span of control afforded to the Are Manager (currently Colin Shearer, fo merly AM Fort William), the area corre ponding to one of the six ScotRa geographical/train service groupings. Th next five years should see completion o the transformation of the Sou'Wes involving the Nith Valley line rational sation, electrification to Ayr and assoc ated resignalling, with steady improve ments to passenger and freight service to/from Stranraer.

Although the Scottish Association fo Public Transport has argued for re instatement of the Dumfries-Stranra line, it would seen impossible to justi two main lines to the port, given th relatively limited investment in track an signalling could increase the capacity (the Ayr-Stranraer line immeasurabl Indeed, as Euan Cameron, Area Manage Ayr until mid-1984 put it: 'the three traf groups — freight, parcels and passenge although impressive, are *needed* to justi a difficult 50-mile stretch of railway'.

carried before the mid-1970s, but from 1,000 cars annually by the late 1970s the total is now seven times that, with consignment of UK-produced and imported vehicles from Dagenham, Harwich, Queenborough and Goole. From two car unloading ramps at Stranraer, cars are discharged by Sealink personnel, some to be conveyed on the company's ferries, others going to a forwarding agent dealing with Cairnryan service. The remaining freight to Stranraer comprises fuel oil for Sealink's ships.

Speedlink trains

All freight services over the Ayr-Stranraer line have been air-braked only since May 1984. At that time, there were three trains each way, two from Tees Yard and one from Carlisle. In mid-1984, another pair of air-braked trains from/to Stranraer was added to cope with the continuing increase in business. There is an imbalance in loaded traffic (outward) so that the four trains from Stranraer convey predominantly empty wagons. One notable recent success to redress the balance was the movement of 1,500 tonnes of Galloway 'Feta' cheese in Interfrigo wagons from the Stockton Haulage terminal to Halkali, Turkey.

Passenger and parcels traffic

Ayr's passenger revenue in 1983 was just under £1million, Stranraer's originating traffic (excluding revenue from Northern Ireland) a quarter of this, Girvan over £90,000, Maybole, £30,000 and Barrhill £11,000. There is no doubt that the daytime Euston-Stranraer trains have had a healthy effect on passenger revenue, as well as providing reasonably attractive journey times to and from Northern Ireland, and in each direction good connections are provided into sailings to/from Larne. Until May 1983, the trains were seasonal but then became all-year-round workings and received Mk 2 d/e sets and Class 47/4 haulage. The overnight Euston trains carry significant Post Office and parcels traffic and the formations may load up to 13 vehicles, including Mk 3 sleeping cars and Mk 2 seating vehicles. From May 1984, the down train was accelerated to an overall

8hr 10min journey, largely by withdrawing intermediate stops. As a result, Barrhill lost its call by the London service, to the accompaniment of indignation locally; to cover it the 18.00 Glasgow-Girvan was later extended to Barrhill.

By the mid-1970s, the Glasgow-Stranraer services were far from attractive and featured the deteriorating Class 126 DMUs working to overall timings of 2¾hr or so. Their immediate replacements as from May 1982 were hardly an improvement. Schedules could not be tightened and the combination of Class 27 locomotives and steam-heated Mk 1 stock was made worse by poor reliability of locomotives and dismal timekeeping.

All this changed from May 1984. The three Stranraer workings each way are no longer timed to fit the interval service north of Ayr and intermediate stops on the northern part of the journey are generally restricted to a Paisley stop in each direction. At the same time, the diagramming of Class 47 motive power, also benefiting from fewer intermediate stops, has allowed the schedule to/from Glasgow to be cut to 2hr 25min and so compete with road coach journeys of 2½hr or so. To emphasise that the service is part of a Scotland-Northern Ireland rail/sea/rail link the Sealink brand image was underlined by the painting of 17 Mk 1 dual-heated coaches in an eyecatching livery of red and about three shades of blue. The Mk 1s were all renovated internally, receiving fluorescent lighting, yellow painted vestibules and refurbished interior panelling. As first outshopped, the effect was startling. Whatever one's views on their technicolour effect (especially alongside DMUs in the Strathclyde PTE colour scheme!) in place of the previously nondescript BR component of the overall service, the stock is now clearly dedicated to the boat trains. Market pricing has been followed to beat the coaches. However, in the face of increased competition, particularly by Ulsterbus, ScotRail has not gained significantly more business, and there may be changes to the present pattern of workings in 1986. Until Class 150 DMUs become available, the Mk 1 stock will remain.

Staple Highland lines motive power: Class 37
No 37.043 *Loch Lomond* approaching Tyndrum
summit with the morning Mallaig-Glasgow
Queen Street passenger train. June 1983.
L. A. Nixon